Christmas Explained

Robins, Kings and Brussel Sprouts

Jonathan Green

SNOWBOOKS

Proudly published by Snowbooks

Snowbooks Ltd
email: info@snowbooks.com
www.snowbooks.com

British Library Cataloguing in Publication Data.
A catalogue record for this book is available from
the British Library.

Hardback: ISBN13 978-1-909679-37-5
Ebook: ISBN13 978-1-909679-41-2

Printed by CPI (UK) Ltd, Croydon, CR0 4YY

Dedication

For Mum, who made Christmases past such a wonderful and memorable time, and for Clare, Jake and Mattie, who mean that Christmas is still something to look forward to today.

A Cornucopia of Christmas Curiosities

Christmastide

"At Christmas play and make good cheer,
For Christmas comes but once a year."

The Christmas that we celebrate today is a creation of the past as much as it is a thing of the present. The customs that we keep are an amalgamation of the practices of other times, cultures, religions and countries. Such diverse groups as the Romans, the Vikings, the peoples of Medieval Europe, and the Victorians, and such faraway places as Germany, Holland, Persia and America have all had as big an impact on the creation and evolution of Christmas as have the birth of the baby Jesus, the Bible and the Holy Land.

Indeed, many of the Christmas customs we keep today have their origins thousands of years before Jesus Christ was even born, when people worshipped the sun as the giver of life. And yet, most of us keep these customs without knowing, or even wondering, why.

Why do we put up Christmas trees, post Christmas

cards, stuff ourselves with turkey and hang up stockings on Christmas Eve? You might answer by saying that it is traditional or simply, because it's Christmas. But how have these traditions come about in the first place? And then there are the fascinating facts about Christmas that have been forgotten in this modern age. Did you know that mince pies were once made with hare's liver, or that Boxing Day was once also called Wren Day?

But let us start at the beginning, with the most obvious, and yet at the same time overlooked, question of all.

Why is Christmas celebrated on 25 December?

Let's clear one thing up before we go any further. Why is Christmas celebrated on 25 December? Well, it's because 25 December is the date of Jesus' birth, isn't it?

No, it isn't. Contrary to popular belief, 25 December is not Jesus Christ's birthday. Oh, and he wasn't born in AD 0 either.

In AD 525, Pope John I charged the scholar Dionysius Exiguus with the task of producing a feast calendar for the Church. Dionysius also estimated the year of

Christ's birth but, due to a number of mistakes in his calculations, he arrived at a date that was a few years shy of the actual event.

So, let's look at the facts.

First of all, the year of Jesus' birth. He was probably born in 6 BC, that's six years before the birth of Christ, believe it or not! Historians have worked this out from the fact that Jesus was born at the time of a Roman census when, 'A decree went out from the Emperor Caesar Augustus that all the world should be taxed'.

The Romans were meticulous about record keeping, as well as making sure that their taxes were collected, and we know that they carried out censuses of the Empire in 20 BC, 6 BC and AD 8. Cross-referencing these with other historical facts, such as the reign of King Herod, it is most likely that 6 BC was the year of Christ's birth. But what of the actual date?

We can't be certain of that, but the best guess that scholars can make is that Jesus was probably born in the spring. The Gospel of Saint Luke relates that when the shepherds were told of Christ's birth, they were, 'out in the fields, keeping watch over their flock by night'. Now, even in the Holy Land, you would not want to be out in the open keeping an eye on your sheep in the middle of winter. This was the sort of thing that would happen in the spring, at lambing time.

It might seem incredible to us now, when 25 December is so linked to celebrating the birth of Christ, but for early Christians Christmas itself was not celebrated in any special way. Little fuss was made of the date, which wasn't even fixed at any particular time of year! For these Christians, the most important time in the Church calendar was Easter, when Christ's conquest of death and subsequent resurrection were celebrated.

Early Christians in fact proposed two entirely different dates for Christ's birth. In the tradition of adapting existing pagan festivals to become Christian ones, some early Christians wanted to celebrate the birth of Jesus on 6 January. This date was proposed by some because it was when the Egyptians observed the festival of the virgin-goddess Kore, while others believed it to be the birthday of Osiris, god of the underworld (and the first Egyptian mummy) who had himself risen again from the dead (albeit with the assistance of his sister-wife Isis).

However, another group wanted to make 25 March the special day on which to commemorate Christ's birth, as this, according to the Ancient Roman calendar, was the date of the spring equinox. This event symbolised the rebirth of the earth, and one Roman writer, Hippolytus (c. AD 170–235), even worked it out to be the anniversary of God's creation of the world itself.

A document supposedly written by one Theophilus of Antioch (AD 171–83) is one of the earliest recognised references to 25 December being the date of Jesus' birth. In the third century AD, 25 December was already a recognised festival, and one that commemorated a special birth. It was the birthday of Mithras, the Persian god of the sun. The cult of Mithras had been brought back to the heart of the Roman Empire by soldiers who had been serving in Syria. There are many surprising similarities between the life of Christ and that of the mythical Mithras.

Mithras was born in a cave, as was Jesus (according to both the *Protoevangelium of James* and *Justin Martyr* from the second century, as this was the typical location of stables in classical Palestine). Mithras sacrificed a bull from the blood of which sprang the whole of creation, just as God, Jesus' father, had created the world. At the end of his life Mithras took part in a feast, just as Jesus took part in the Last Supper, before being taken up into heaven in a fiery chariot, just as Jesus ascended to heaven after his resurrection from the dead.

Nonetheless, it wasn't until the year AD 350 that the then Pope, Julius I, made it official. He decreed that Christ's birth would be celebrated on 25 December, because it would make it as easy as possible for those Romans who were still pagans (which was most of them) to make the change to the new rituals. The first official mention of there being a Feast of the Nativity on 25 December is in a document known as the Philocalian Calendar, dating from AD 354, but which makes reference to an older document from AD 336. So we at least know that by 354 the celebration of Christmas had become an annual event.

But what of our name for this festival; where did that come from? The first written reference we have to the word 'Christmas' itself being used comes from a Saxon book which mentions *Cristes Maesse*, meaning 'Christ's Mass' from where we get 'Christmas'.

Christmas itself is pre-dated by two major pagan festivals, the Roman Saturnalia and the Viking Yule. Saturnalia was characterized by its turning of the established order on its head, with servants becoming the masters and vice versa. Its legacy lived on in the Medieval Christmas when a Lord of Misrule was appointed to oversee the often noisy and disorderly festive celebrations.

It is thought that these midwinter festivals were transformed into Christmas celebrations after the arrival of Saint Augustine in England, at the end of the sixth century, and the subsequent widespread adoption of Christianity by the British. Certainly Christmas Day AD 598 was marked by a spectacular event, when

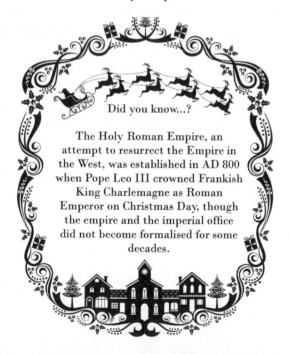

Did you know...?

The Holy Roman Empire, an attempt to resurrect the Empire in the West, was established in AD 800 when Pope Leo III crowned Frankish King Charlemagne as Roman Emperor on Christmas Day, though the empire and the imperial office did not become formalised for some decades.

more than 10,000 Englishmen were baptised as Christians.

Some pagan customs were adopted by Christianity in part to help people accept the new religion and convert to it willingly, it being easier and less antagonistic to apply Christian meanings and symbolism to the old rituals rather than try to simply stamp them out.

So, apart from the Persian sun god Mithras, who else was born on Christmas Day? Well, according to the law of averages, plenty of people have been denied the pleasure of receiving presents twice a year, by having their birthday fall on 25 December. However, among the more well-known are the scientist and mathematician Sir Isaac Newton (1642), the American actor Humphrey Bogart (1899), the author Quentin Crisp (1908), the comedian Kenny Everett (1945), the singer Annie Lennox (1954), Shane McGowan (1957) whose name will always be associated with Christmas thanks to his penning of *Fairytale of New York*, and the pop star Dido Florian Cloud de Bounevialle Armstrong (1971), who is better known as just Dido.

If you, or someone close to you, should ever happen to become the bearer of glad tidings one Christmas Day, or at least the parent of a seasonal bundle of joy, you could always consider blessing the baby with one of the following festive names: Noel, Carol, Joy, Holly, Eve, Nicholas, Merry, Rudolph, or if it's twins, Cinnamon and Ginger!

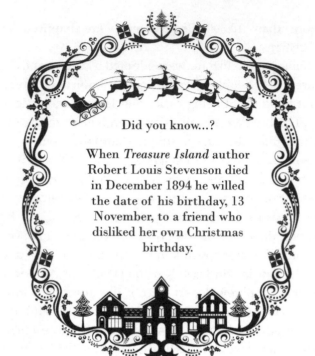

Did you know...?

When *Treasure Island* author Robert Louis Stevenson died in December 1894 he willed the date of his birthday, 13 November, to a friend who disliked her own Christmas birthday.

The A to Z of Christmas

A

is for Angels

A traditional part of many a parent's Christmas is the school Nativity Play and what would the Nativity Play be without the child – dressed in a white smock and wearing a tinsel halo – playing the part of the Archangel Gabriel?

The role of Gabriel is rather like that of the Pantomime Dame or Principal Boy, in that it is a gender reversal role; Gabriel is male but is more often than not played by a girl. And it is because of the vital part they play in the Christmas story that angels have become so associated with the festive season.

The word 'angel' comes from a Greek word meaning 'messenger'. In the Bible, angels are represented as immortal, divine beings, who act as intermediaries between God and humankind. Traditionally, pictures and poems about angels portray them as having human bodies with wings sprouting from their backs. The wings are said to symbolize innocence, virtue, purity, peace and love, qualities which taken together place the angels above humans, although they are still under God.

Nine ranks of angels are recorded in the Bible, with Seraphim and Cherubim being at the top of the rankings, as it were. Within this heavenly hierarchy, the chief angels are the Archangels Gabriel and Michael. However, it is interesting to note that Christian doctrine about angels evolved most rapidly between the years AD 1100-1200. (An example of this change in theological thought can be seen in the teachings of Saint Thomas Aquinas.)

Angels were, of course, instrumental in the birth of Jesus Christ and hence play an important part in Christmas celebrations and festivities. It was the Archangel Gabriel who told Mary she was to bear

God's son. Another angel informed Joseph that he should marry Mary and look after the Christ child. Angels were the ones that brought the news of Christ's birth to the wider world, via the shepherds keeping watch over their flocks by night.

According to one particularly twee legend, God appointed a small group of tiny angels, who were just learning their angel ways, to watch over Joseph and Mary on their journey to Bethlehem. These tiny angels did the best they could but failed to help the couple find shelter in the infamously over-crowded inn, so the Holy Family were forced to make do with the stable. Nonetheless, these tiny angels were so excited that they were to witness the birth of God's Only Son that they flew closer to the Earth and sang sweetly. The fastest among them caught sight of the newborn child from the stable's roof and instantly understood their mission was to herald the birth. They were so filled with joy and mirth that they burst into a glorious thanksgiving song that reached the heavens and was so melodious that it could be heard all over the Earth.

Why is turkey eaten at Christmas?

What would Christmas dinner be without roast turkey and all the trimmings? (And what would the days following Christmas be like without the endless rounds of turkey sandwiches?) But how did a bird which is not native to Britain become the most intrinsic element of all the festive fare?

Did you know...?

A female domesticated turkey is called a 'hen' and its chick is a 'poult'. In the United States, the male turkey is referred to as a 'tom', whereas it Europe it is known as a 'stag'.

The turkey originally came from Mexico – not Turkey – and was brought back by Spanish adventurers. The bird was introduced into central Europe by Turkish traders and so became known as the turkey-cock, or simply turkey. However, just to confuse things even more, the turkey was sometimes known as the Indian peacock (which it even stranger when you consider that India is where the peacock itself originally came from)!

The confusion regarding its origins – and hence the bird's name – stemmed from the fact that when Christopher Columbus and his friends first discovered the Americas they were actually looking for an alternative route to India and the East. In their confusion they believed, at first, that they had found India, which is why the West Indies are so named.

In other European countries this confusion over the turkey's origins was reflected in its name. In France the turkey was called *coq d'Inde* (now corrupted to *dinde*), in Italy it was the *galle d'India*, in Germany its name was *indianische henn*, while throughout the Ottoman Empire it was called the *hindi*.

The turkey arrived in Britain some time after 1510 so has actually been with us for nearly 500 years. From the sixteenth century, turkeys were reared in Norfolk, which still has strong connections to the bird. For many years the coming of autumn saw an annual migration of turkeys from East Anglia to London, as drovers walked them to market.

Thousands of the birds would be herded to London in this way. The turkeys averaged only one mile a day, but this would, nonetheless, have soon made them lame – were it not for the fact that to overcome that very problem the farmers tarred their feet or, in some cases, even provided them with little leather boots!

But even before the arrival of the turkey in the British Isles, poultry was still an important part of the Christmas menu. There were, after all, plenty of native British birds to dine upon, everything from peacock, plover and pheasant to capons, woodcock and swan!

It was the fashionable practice at court to present the birds as if they were still alive, sitting up on the platter as if they were quite happy that they were about to be

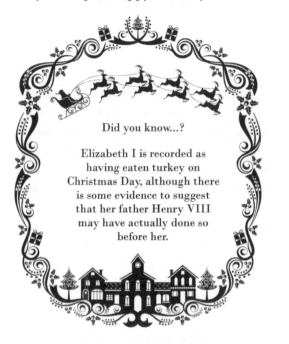

Did you know...?

Elizabeth I is recorded as having eaten turkey on Christmas Day, although there is some evidence to suggest that her father Henry VIII may have actually done so before her.

eaten. To achieve this effect, a bird would be skinned with the utmost care (rather than plucked) before it was cooked. Once the bird had been roasted over the fire, its skin would be replaced and the cuts that had been made to remove it in the first place sewn up again.

Roast swan, was another popular dish among the aristocracy that was presented in this way. There were many different ways of preparing and serving swan. Here is just one of them.

Roast swan

1 swan

Olive oil

First clean and gut your swan, then cover the outside of the bird with olive oil. Roast it on a spit or, failing that, in the oven. Baste frequently with its own juice and when it is done carve and serve in pieces.

If that's too plain for you, then you can make a Chaudon sauce to accompany the bird, but for this you'll need to have saved the swan's giblets.

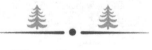

Chaudon sauce

Swan giblets

Red wine vinegar

Broth

Toasted breadcrumbs

Salt

Ginger

Galingale

Start by washing the giblets. While they're still wet, salt them, before placing in a pot. Cover the giblets with water and boil. Once they're done, drain and cool, before cutting into small pieces. Combine the chopped giblets, breadcrumbs, spices and broth in a food blender and whizz them up until the whole lot forms a smooth sauce. Bring to the boil in another pan, simmer and add a little of the red wine vinegar to give it a sharp bite. Serve with the swan.

(In case you're wondering, *Galingale* is another plant of the Ginger family.)

Before heading down to the local butcher's to ask for swan, though, you should bear in mind that all swans are protected under the Wildlife and Countryside Act of 1981. The mute swan, however, is even better protected because the species is owned by the Crown, and has been ever since 1482. A small number of shooting licences are granted to farmers each year, *if* they can prove that swans have damaged their crops, but in all other cases it is an offence to be in possession of a swan carcass, even if the bird died of natural causes!

The same treatment of dressing the roast bird in its own skin would have been applied to the peacock, another dish that was the preserve of the wealthy. In this case, the bird was presented with its full tail and its head crest and beak covered with gold leaf. A final touch was to put a wick inside the bird's beak which would then be lit just before it was brought to the table. However, some Medieval foodies felt that although it was supposed to be a delicacy, the peacock, like so many other wild birds, didn't actually taste very nice. They therefore suggested sewing a roast goose up inside the peacock's skin instead, to make the dish more palatable.

Goose was the most popular bird eaten by the smaller households at Christmas time, with chicken and capon popular alternatives. Such domesticated fowl were, of course, more readily available. However, in the north of the country, it wasn't goose but roast beef that was the meat of choice for Christmas dinner.

The Victorians had a goose club, which was a savings club. By saving a little each week you eventually had enough to buy a goose to eat on Christmas Day. In Charles Dickens' *A Christmas Carol*, the Cratchit family were preparing to sit down to enjoy a Christmas goose before Ebenezer Scrooge bought them the best turkey in the shop.

The growth of industrialised farming has helped to make turkey many people's first choice for Christmas dinner, as it is now very cheap to produce, while the bird itself offers the consumer a large amount of meat for their money. Before the Second World War turkey was still something of a luxury as far as most British households were concerned.

And what would any roast poultry – whether goose, chicken, turkey or peacock – be without stuffing. The term 'stuffing' didn't appear until 1538; before that time it was called forcemeat and, unsurprisingly, its list of ingredients is slightly different from what we know as stuffing today.

Did you know...?

Samuel Pepys – that font of so much seventeenth century social knowledge – wrote of a sauce to accompany turkey, the recipe for which was invented by the then Duke of York (later to become King James II). It was, 'made from parsley and dry toast beat together in a mortar, together with vinegar, salt and a little pepper' and sounds not unlike a parsley and breadcrumbs stuffing.

Forcemeat

175 g/6 oz breadcrumbs
100 g/4 oz suet
50 g/2 oz ham (or lean bacon)

1 onion
2 eggs
1 tsp parsley, minced
1 tsp sweet herbs, minced
½ a lemon, rind only
Salt

Cayenne

Pounded mace

Olive oil (or lard)

To make enough forcemeat to accompany one turkey, start by shredding the ham (or bacon); chop the suet with the lemon rind and the herbs, making sure that everything is finely minced. Mince the onion just as finely and add this too. Add some salt, cayenne and mace, and blend it all together with the breadcrumbs.

Take the eggs, beat them and then strain them, and finally mix them with the other ingredients. Shape the forcemeat into balls before frying them in olive oil (or lard, if you're after a more authentic flavour). An alternative to frying is to place the forcemeat balls on a baking tray, before baking them for 30 minutes in a moderate oven.

There are some who believe that the recognised antiseptic properties of herbs such as thyme, marjoram and sage, as used in stuffing could have helped offset any nasty side effects of eating badly cooked or slightly dodgy poultry. However, there are more reasons for it becoming an important part of the Christmas meal.

Firstly, the addition of stuffing helped to make the meat go further and fill up the stomachs of hungry diners. Secondly, putting the stuffing inside the bird helped it to keep its shape during cooking, and even

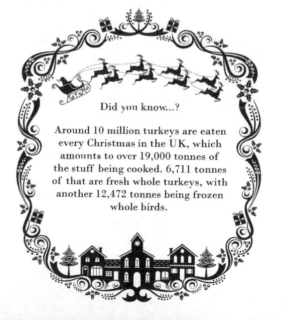

Did you know...?

Around 10 million turkeys are eaten every Christmas in the UK, which amounts to over 19,000 tonnes of the stuff being cooked. 6,711 tonnes of that are fresh whole turkeys, with another 12,472 tonnes being frozen whole birds.

made it easier for the carcass to stay on the spit while it was being roasted over the fire.

However, despite the fact that turkey had been on Christmas menus for so long, up until 1851 Queen Victoria still ate swan for Christmas dinner. Then, when she did get turned on to turkey, she (or rather her cooks) really went to town. The turkey was roasted in a rich pastry and stuffed with three other birds! Inside the turkey was a chicken, inside that was a pheasant and lastly, inside that, was a woodcock, all with their bones removed – for convenience, of course.

But four birds baked together was nothing compared to the legendary ten-bird roast championed by celebrity chef Hugh Fearnley-Whittingstall. A turkey is stuffed with a goose, duck, mallard, guinea fowl, chicken, pheasant, partridge, pigeon and woodcock. When cooked it weighs 22lb and contains around 10,000 calories (the average turkey contains 3,000 calories). It also takes over nine hours to prepare and cook.

But if all this talk of turkey has got you thinking along the lines of 'What's the perfect way to roast my Christmas turkey this year?' then look no further.

FOR You!

26

Christmas Turkey

1 oven-ready turkey
150 g/6 oz softened butter
200 g/8 oz bacon
1 lemon
6 bay leaves
Salt and pepper

Christmas Stuffing

2 large onions
1 tbs dried sage
85 g/3 oz dried apricots
85 g/3 oz dried cranberries
900 g/2 lb pork sausage meat
4 tbs white breadcrumbs
1 egg
Salt and pepper

Preheat the oven to 220°C and while you're doing that, make the stuffing. In a large bowl combine the breadcrumbs with the sage and one of the onions (finely minced), adding a little boiling water before mixing thoroughly.

Next in goes the dried fruit; give it another stir. Then add the sausage meat and egg to the mixture, adding a little salt and pepper to taste.

Stuff the turkey with the stuffing, pushing it into the neck end and tucking the neck flap back under the turkey. The rest of the stuffing then goes into the body cavity along with one whole, peeled onion.

Place the turkey in a deep roasting dish. Smother it with the softened butter combined with the zest of the lemon. Layer the slices of bacon on top, using them to keep the bay leaves next to the skin.

When it comes to actually roasting the bird you need to allow 20 minutes per 1lb, cooking it for another 20 minutes on top of that. A 14lb bird will feed fourteen people comfortably.

Traditional accompaniments for roast turkey are both cranberry sauce and bread sauce. Cranberry sauce was once restricted to northern rural areas, where wild cranberries grew in abundance. In the south, or the cities, until cranberries became more readily available towards the end of the 20th century, bread sauce had to suffice. Sausages wrapped in bacon – also known by the rather twee term 'pigs in blankets' – are also served with the bird.

Where does the Christmas tree come from?

It would be hard to imagine Christmas without the familiar conical form of the festive tree. From December onwards (if not before) they can be found everywhere, from homes and schools to department stores and pretty much anywhere people will spend any amount of time during the Christmas period, whether it be a hospital or an office block. But where does the tradition of putting up a tree indoors come from, and has it always been such an important part of the Christmas celebrations as we know them?

Well, in some ways it is one of the more recently-established Christmas traditions, with the decorated tree as we know it rising to popularity during Queen Victoria's reign. And then, in other ways, the tradition is older than Christmas itself.

At its root, it is really just another example of an evergreen brought into the home during the cold dark days of winter by our pagan forebears, along with the Yule log, boughs of holly and mistletoe. But it was actually the Romans who got there first, as they did with so much that has become modern-day Christmas tradition. During the festival of Saturnalia, held in honour of Saturn, the god of agriculture, Ancient Romans decorated trees with small pieces of metal.

The first Christmas trees were decorated with apples, as a symbol of Man's fall in the Garden of Eden when Adam and Eve ate of the fruit of tree of knowledge. As a result, they were called Paradise trees. In time other decorations were added, in the form of nuts and even red ribbons, or strips of paper. Ultimately the apples were replaced by Christmas baubles.

In the Middle Ages, the Paradise tree went up on the feast day dedicated to Adam and Eve, 24 December, and to this day, purists believe that you should wait until Christmas Eve to erect your own tree, and then take it down again on Twelfth Night.

Possibly the earliest depiction of a Christmas tree dates from 1521 and comes from Germany. The painting shows a procession of musicians accompanying a horse-riding holy man – who may be a bishop or even Saint Nicholas – parading through a town. One of the men in the procession is holding high a tree decorated with what look like apples.

A candle-lit fir was also erected in a London street in the fifteenth century, but such trees remained as outside decorations and there are no records from the time stating that they were ever taken into the home. Evergreens in other forms were used to decorate houses though, so it is quite possible that some homes also included a tree, rather than simply being adorned with bits of one.

However, according to some historians the first recorded mention of an actual Christmas tree appears in a diary from Strasbourg, dated 1605. This particular tree was decorated with paper roses, apples, sweets and gold foil – the first tinsel.

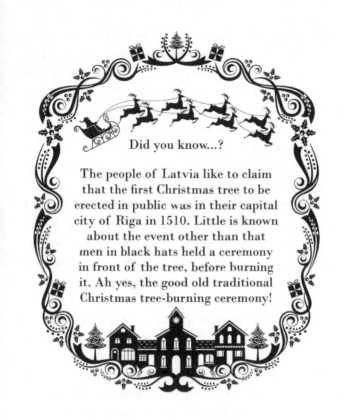

In the Church's attempts to Christianise what was
essentially a pagan practice, the Christmas fir had
Christian symbolism foisted upon it. Since to look at
it, its shape was essentially triangular, the three points
of the triangle were said to represent the Holy Trinity –
God the Father, God the Son and God the Holy Spirit.

To add weight to the argument that putting up a tree
in your house during the winter months was their idea,
Christians in the Middle Ages also perpetuated the
legend of Saint Boniface, which pre-dated Germanic

31

diary references to Christmas trees by several hundred years. Boniface was a monk (and schoolmaster) from Devon, living in the seventh and eighth centuries, but the event that connects him with the origins of the Christmas tree occurred at Geismar, in Germany. He was there carrying out missionary work, preaching the gospel, at the behest of Pope Gregory II.

The story goes that Boniface came upon a group of pagans worshipping a sacred oak tree. The druids were preparing to sacrifice a baby to their bloodthirsty pagan gods when Saint Boniface came to the infant's rescue. Incensed, he grabbed the axe that was going to be used to end to the baby's life and instead laid into the tree, furiously chopping it down. With the babe safe in his arms, he saw that from the roots of the felled oak a fir tree was growing. To his holy eyes the fir was a symbol of Christ's resurrection, with new life growing out of what had been a tree of death.

Sometimes this story is linked to a different saint, the seventh century Wilfrid of York. In this version the saint set out to cut down an oak tree which was the focus of a druidic cult. As he chopped it down, the oak split and a fir tree grew from its heart. Wilfrid dedicated the fir to Christ, declaring that the evergreen represented the eternal life offered by the Saviour.

And then again sixteenth century folklore states that it was Martin Luther, the German theologian, who was the first person to bring a decorated tree into the home. After walking through a star-lit forest of evergreens, Martin felt inspired. Bringing a tree into his own home and illuminating it with candles, he reminded his family that Jesus Christ himself had descended from Heaven to die for our sins. However, there are some historians who claim that there is no evidence of a lighted tree until more than a century after Martin Luther's death in 1546.

Did you know...?

According to the Royal Society for the Prevention of Accidents, there are 1,000 Christmas tree related A&E visits every year in the UK.

It is the commonly held belief that it was Prince Albert, consort of her majesty Queen Victoria, who first brought a tree – in this case ordered from Coburg in Germany – into the home – in this case Windsor Castle – at Christmas time. However, although it may be true that the tree he had set up for his family in 1841 set the trend for such trees – after the Royal Family were depicted gathered around the royal Christmas tree in the London Illustrated News of 1848 – this wasn't the first time Windsor Castle had had a tree.

Queen Charlotte, the German consort of King George III and Victoria's grandmother, had ordered a Christmas tree, or *Weihnachtsbaum*, for the Queen's lodge at Windsor in 1800, and trees became a permanent fixture there for a number of years afterwards. The practice had been a common one in Germany, before the Royal Family popularised it in the UK.

Nowadays, you will find Christmas trees all over the country, particularly in London. However, the largest tree you will see on display in the capital is the one given to the city of Westminster each year by the people of Oslo in Norway, in gratitude for the help Norway received from Britain during the Second World War, when the Scandinavian country was occupied by enemy forces. King Haakon of Norway escaped to England and set up the Free Norwegian Government. Every year since 1947 the Norwegian tree has been put on display in Trafalgar Square. At approximately 70 feet tall, it is the only un-milled tree over twelve feet that is allowed to be imported into the country.

Did you know...?

According to the Guinness Book of World Records, the largest human Christmas tree was made up of 1,982 participants and was achieved by the Fiesta Nacional de la Navidad in Argentina, on 29 November 2013.

The most expensively dressed Christmas tree was valued at 41,329,531 AED (£6,975,880). It was erected by the Emirates Palace in Abu Dhabi, in the United Arab Emirates, and displayed from 16-29 December 2010. The tree stood 13.1 m (43.2 ft) high and was covered in 181 individual items of jewellery.

is for Bees

Many people are familiar with the various traditions associated with Christmas Eve but there are a number of older legends that have been forgotten over time. One of these is specifically associated with midnight on Christmas Eve. It is at this time that bees supposedly hum their own hymn in praise of Christ.

There are a number of other superstitions concerning bees. If a bee enters your home it is said to be a sign that you will soon have a visitor (other than the bee, of course). If you kill the bee, you will bring bad luck down upon yourself, or the visitor will be particularly unpleasant. And it gets worse; a swarm of bees settling on a roof is a sure sign that the house will burn down!

Who were the Three Kings?

In the traditional Christmas story, acted out in Nativity plays year in year out around the country, the infant Jesus is visited by three kings who present him with expensive gifts full of symbolic meaning. But who actually were this trio of monarchs?

Well, this is something of an academic question really as, according to scholars of the Bible, they weren't kings and there weren't three of them. For starters, of the four gospels in the Bible – those written by Matthew, Mark, Luke and John – only two mention anything about Christ's birth. And then, just to complicate matters, Matthew and Luke – who did write about the Nativity – provide us with different parts of what has become the traditional Christmas story. Luke tells us about the shepherds and hosts of angels, while Matthew relates the part where the wise men come to worship the Christ child, and the holy family's resulting escape from the paranoid, not to say sociopathic, King Herod.

It is also interesting to note that the story of Jesus' birth was not as important to early Christians as his teachings or the events surrounding his death. Of the 27 books in the New Testament, only two mention anything about the Nativity, and then only briefly. However, in our secular modern world, for many Christmas is the only Christian festival that is uniformly celebrated on any kind of scale.

But back to the kings... this is what Matthew has to say about the wise men's visit:

> After Jesus was born in Bethlehem in Judea,
> during the time of King Herod, wise men from
> the East came to Jerusalem and asked, 'Where
> is the one who has been born king of the Jews?
> We saw his star in the east and have come to
> worship him'. (Matthew 2:1–2)

At this point, the Bible seems clear that the baby Jesus' visitors were wise men. However, in some sources, these visitors are described as Magi, astrologers-cum-astronomers-cum-religious sages. In fact, those who are knowledgeable about such matters agree that the Magi were Zoroastrian astrologer-priests, not kings. And there weren't three of them either.

Scholars still debate whether there were in fact only two wise men. (As they are mentioned in the plural we know there have to have been at least two.) Others argue it was more like twenty, while Eastern tradition claims there were twelve. The familiar figure of three wasn't settled on by the Church until the sixth century.

It would appear that the confusion over the number of wise men came about because what the Bible *does* mention is that these far-ranging holy men brought the infant Christ three gifts. Early interpreters of the Bible, perhaps understandably, took this to mean that each gift had been given by one individual; hence three wise men.

This confusion may have been strengthened by the fact that in Psalm 72, kings from three different places – Tarshish, Sheba and Seba – brought tribute to King Solomon and knelt before him (probably swearing fealty, as Solomon was effectively the superpower of his time in that part of the world).

And there is a third Biblical source which has helped create the traditional image of the three kings; that of the Book of Isaiah. It is Isaiah who prophesies Jesus' birth. Isaiah Chapter 60 also mentions gold and frankincense, two of the three gifts which Matthew says the wise men brought to Jesus, the last being myrrh. And the prophet also mentions both kings and camels, although Matthew does not.

So you can see how these references became jumbled together to create the image of the three kings that is a mainstay of Nativity plays to this day.

Thanks to the popular Christmas carol 'We Three Kings' (actually properly titled 'Kings of Orient') most people are familiar with the fact that the three kings' names were Melchior, Caspar and Balthazar. But if there weren't actually three kings, how did these names become associated with them?

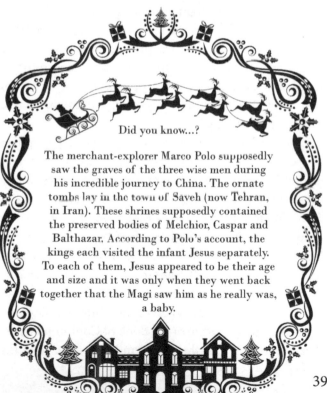

Did you know...?

The merchant-explorer Marco Polo supposedly saw the graves of the three wise men during his incredible journey to China. The ornate tombs lay in the town of Saveh (now Tehran, in Iran). These shrines supposedly contained the preserved bodies of Melchior, Caspar and Balthazar. According to Polo's account, the kings each visited the infant Jesus separately. To each of them, Jesus appeared to be their age and size and it was only when they went back together that the Magi saw him as he really was, a baby.

The first literary source that mentions the names of the three is a chronicle dating from the sixth century called the *Excerpta Latina Barbari*. In it, the chronicler mentions the birth of Jesus and later goes on to say that, 'the Magi brought him gifts and venerated him. The Magi are called Bithisarea, Melchior and Gaspar'.

The more common spelling of Bithisarea was Balthazar, and Balthazar was a corruption of Belteshazzar – which was the name by which the prophet Daniel (as in the lions' den) was known at the Babylonian court. It is likely that the name Melchior is formed from the Hebrew words *melek* (meaning 'king') and *or* (meaning 'light'), making him the King of Light. As such he was the king who brought the baby Jesus a gift of gold, after the precious metal's dazzling brightness. Caspar, or Gaspar, may be a corruption of Godaphar. A character who appears in an apocryphal text known as the *Act of Thomas*, Godaphar was a famous Indian king.

It was a later written reference, which is found in the *Collectanea* (a book probably from Ireland and probably dating from the eighth century), which finally crystallised the now familiar image of three dignitaries from foreign lands. It has Melchior, the bringer of gold, as an old man with a white beard. Caspar, the bringer of frankincense, in contrast is seen as young and beardless, while Balthasar, the bringer of myrrh, is African and has a black beard.

In 2004, the General Synod of the Church of England consented to a revision of the Book of Common Prayer. A committee agreed that the term Magi, as used in the

Bible, was the name used by officials at the Persian court. This means that not only were Jesus' visiting Magi not kings, did not number three and were possibly not even wise, they might have been female as well!

is for Christmas Star

In Christian tradition, the Christmas Star – also called the Star of Bethlehem – revealed the birthplace of Jesus to the magi. The star appears in the nativity story of the Gospel of Matthew, where Magi "from the east" are inspired by the star to travel to Jerusalem. The star eventually leads them to Jesus' house in Bethlehem, where they pay him homage, worship him, and bestow their gifts upon him.

Many Christians see the star as a miraculous sign to mark Christ's birth. Some theologians claim that the star fulfilled a prophecy, known as the Star Prophecy, while astronomers have made several attempts to link the star to unusual astronomical events. Current contenders for the Star of Bethlehem include for following:

1) A series of three conjunctions of the planets Jupiter

and Saturn occurred in the year 7 BC (proposed by the German astronomer Johannes Kepler in 1614). However, modern calculations show that there was a gap of nearly a degree between the planets, so these conjunctions were not visually impressive.

2) An astronomical event where Jupiter and Saturn were in a triple conjunction in the constellation Pisces (as argued by Dr. Karlis Kaufmanis in the twentieth century).

3) A comet. Halley's Comet was visible in 12 BC and another object, possibly a comet or nova, was seen by Chinese and Korean stargazers in around 5 BC. This object was observed for over seventy days with no movement recorded. Also, ancient writers described comets as "hanging over" specific cities, just as the Star of Bethlehem was said to have "stood over" the place where Jesus was in the town of Bethlehem. However, in ancient times comets were generally seen as bad omens.

4) Uranus, which passed close to Saturn in 9 BC and Venus in 6 BC. However, this is unlikely because Uranus moves very slowly and is barely visible with the naked eye.

What is myrrh anyway?

Everybody has heard of gold, frankincense and myrrh in the context of the Christmas story. They were, of course, the gifts brought to the baby Jesus by the three wise men. There probably isn't anyone who doesn't know what gold is (a relatively rare, shiny yellow metal, chemical symbol 'Au') but what of frankincense and, to quote the classic *Monty Python's Life of Brian*, 'What is myrrh anyway?'

Of the two, it is frankincense which is the better known. It is a type of incense made from the aromatic resin of the *Boswellia* tree. It was introduced to Europe by Frankish crusaders, hence its name, and used lavishly in religious rituals.When blocks of the hardened resin are burnt, the frankincense gives off a sweet-smelling smoke.

Myrrh is also a type of incense. *Commiphora myrrha* is a thorny shrub native to Somalia and the eastern reaches of Ethiopia, in Africa. Today, it can also be found growing in other parts of the world, particularly the Arabian Peninsula, as it has been introduced to these regions over the years. However, at the time of Christ's birth part of what made myrrh so valuable was the distances that had to be travelled to get hold of the stuff.

Myrrh, as it would have been given to the infant Jesus, is the dried sap of the shrub, a resinous material, reddish-brown in colour. The clearer the resin and the darker it is, the better the quality. The scent of raw myrrh is sharp and pleasant but also slightly bitter. The smoke it produces when burnt is also quite bitter, but it also has a sweet, tarry odour, with notes of vanilla.

Its enduring connection has always been with funerals and cremations, hence its prophetic significance as one of the gifts given to Jesus. Up until the fifteenth century it was used as an embalming ointment.

Each of the three gifts given to the Christ child by the wise men had symbolic significance. Gold was a symbol of kingship and glory, but also of Christ's divinity. Frankincense, as the perfume used in ritual worship, stood for both purity and ascending prayer, and spoke of Christ's godhead and godliness. Myrrh, the fragrant burial ointment, was a symbol of Christ's mortality, foretelling his death on the cross, and ultimately his resurrection.

Both myrrh and frankincense are collected in the same way. Delicate incisions are made into the bark of the tree using a special tool. The milky sap that exudes from these incisions hardens as soon as it comes into contact with the air, forming 'tears' which are then collected a fortnight later. This process is called 'tapping'. Once collected, the resin is stored for twelve weeks, giving it time to harden completely. All that happens after this is that the globules of resin are sorted and graded, a process usually undertaken by the merchant buying it from the collector.

Gum resins were first collected in this way in Arabia, a region which one ancient chronicler, Diodorus Siculus, described as exuding, 'a most delicate fragrance; even the sailors passing by Arabia can smell the strong fragrance that gives health and vigour'.

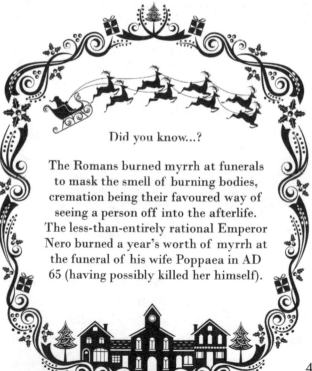

Did you know...?

The Romans burned myrrh at funerals to mask the smell of burning bodies, cremation being their favoured way of seeing a person off into the afterlife. The less-than-entirely rational Emperor Nero burned a year's worth of myrrh at the funeral of his wife Poppaea in AD 65 (having possibly killed her himself).

Myrrh was highly prized in Ancient times and was literally worth more than its weight in gold. In Ancient Rome it cost five times as much as frankincense, although the latter was by far the more popular.

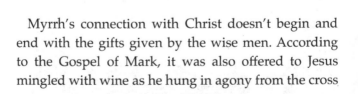

Did you know...?

Myrrh is put to a wide variety of uses in traditional Chinese medicine. It is supposed to help alleviate toothache, and is used as a liniment for bruises, aches and sprains. It is also prescribed for rheumatic, arthritic and circulatory problems. However, most amazing of all, according to Western herbalism it is supposed to have the power to make you younger-looking again!

Myrrh's connection with Christ doesn't begin and end with the gifts given by the wise men. According to the Gospel of Mark, it was also offered to Jesus mingled with wine as he hung in agony from the cross at his crucifixion, the intention being to numb the pain he was feeling. This practice of using myrrh as an additive to wine was common in the Ancient world and has even lasted to this day in certain parts of the globe. Myrrh was also used to anoint Jesus' body after his death.

You probably wouldn't be surprised to learn that something so rare and highly valued in ages past is much more widely available today. However, you might be surprised to discover that it is quite possible that you have some lying around the house yourself. It is found in everything from perfumes and lotions to toothpastes and mouthwashes; its antiseptic properties help treat and prevent gum disease. Nursing mothers have known of its analgesic properties for a long time as well, rubbing it onto babies' gums to relieve the pain they feel when teething.

As well as its connections with Christmas through the story of the Nativity, myrrh also has a link to Father Christmas – or at least the fourth century bishop Saint Nicholas who inspired the festive gift-giver. It was said that healing myrrh flowed from the saint's sacred relics. Pilgrims seeking such miraculous healing at his shrine would pray to Saint Nicholas as follows:

> With divine myrrh the divine grace of the Spirit anointed thee, who didst preside as the leader of Myra, and having made the ends of the world fragrant with the myrrh of virtues, thou holiest of men, through the pleasant breathings of thine intercessions always driving away the evil stench of the passions.

Therefore, in faith we render thee great praise, and celebrate thine all-holy memory, O Nicholas.

Did you know...?

In Russia, in 1998, two icons associated with Tsar Nicholas II were reported as streaming myrrh, letting off a gentle flow of it each day. When this curious phenomenon was investigated further, both icons were found to have once been kept at a church dedicated to Saint Nicholas.

Why are cards sent at Christmas?

For many people, the festive season really gets under way with the sending and receiving of their first Christmas cards, usually some time in November! It is an annual burden, writing endless cards to be sent to people who you last had contact with twelve months before, when you last received a card from them, but it is one that we would not be without.

Because the giving and receiving of cards is so inextricably linked to Christmas, it is hard to imagine a time when we didn't have Christmas cards. But of course something else we take for granted these days is the postal service. Without a postal service there would be no way of sending all those sackloads of cards, and a reliable (and, more importantly, affordable) postal service wasn't created until the mid-1800s. As a result, the greeting card didn't appear until the Victorian era either.

That said, the exchanging of illustrated greetings cards on special occasions itself can be traced back to the Romans and even the Ancient Egyptians before them. Of course, these weren't Christmas cards as we know them, but we came a step closer in the fifteenth century when British engravers began printing special Christmas pictures to sell during the festive period. However, these pictures came complete with New Year's greetings rather than Christmas ones.

Early in Queen Victoria's reign, it was a popular practice for people to send hand-drawn 'Christmas sheets' to their friends and family. These were pictures, on single sheets of paper, with space left for the sender to add his or her name. It also became popular at this time for the more well-to-do members of society to add a printed Christmas message to the calling cards they presented on visiting the house of another well-to-do person.

However, the first true commercial Christmas card – one that we would recognise as being just that – didn't go on sale until 1843. It was printed at the behest of Sir Henry Cole, a businessman and philanthropist, who had played a key role in introducing the Penny Post in 1840 (and who would go on to be the chief organiser of the Great Exhibition of 1851). Thanks to the Penny Post, it was possible to send a letter or card anywhere within Britain. Director of the newly founded Victoria and Albert Museum in London, it was also Cole who came up with the idea of perforated edges for stamps.

Cole commissioned artist John Callcott Horsley to produce the image for the front, which showed a family party, along with vignettes of people carrying out charitable acts for the poor. It also bore the festive message, 'A Merry Christmas and a Happy New Year to You!' The card was printed by Jobbins of Warwick Court, Holborn. The black and white card then had to be hand-coloured. The cards sold for a shilling each and Cole managed to shift nearly 1,000.

The Christmas card had arrived, and it was an instant hit! The Victorians being Victorians, it wasn't long before Christmas cards became more elaborate. Soon there were pop-up cards which opened out into incredible 3D scenes, and ones which implemented cunning techniques to make a character appear to climb out of the card.

By the 1860s Christmas cards were being mentioned in publications such as *Punch* magazine and *The Times* newspaper. Although they started off with flowery borders and pretty lace edging, soon what we would consider to be more traditional Christmas scenes had begun to appear on the cards. For example, the robin (a perennial favourite) first appeared on a card in 1862. Other popular subject matter included Father Christmas in his sleigh, holly, mistletoe, Christmas trees, Nativity scenes, candles, and angels. However, the first American Christmas card showed Santa and a slave laying a table. God bless America!

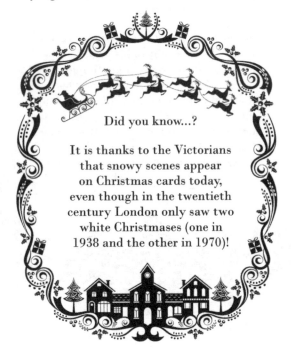

Did you know...?

It is thanks to the Victorians that snowy scenes appear on Christmas cards today, even though in the twentieth century London only saw two white Christmases (one in 1938 and the other in 1970)!

In 1880, the Post Office made its first ever plea to 'Post early for Christmas'. Nearly ten years prior to this, in 1871, one newspaper complained that the delivery of business mail was being delayed because of the sheer volume of Christmas cards piling up in post offices.

By 1873 people had started publishing adverts in newspapers wishing their friends all the very best for the festive season and stating that they would not be sending Christmas cards that year.

Did you know...?

Every year, more than 1.8 billion Christmas cards are sent within the United Kingdom. To make all of these cards, over 200,000 trees have to be felled. But it's all for a good cause – charities estimate that £50 million is raised for good causes through the sales of charity Christmas cards each year.

However, the Christmas card created by scientists at the University of Glasgow in 2010 didn't require the felling of any trees. Measuring only 200 micrometres by 290 micrometres, recipients would have needed a high-powered microscope to read them, and 8,276 of the cards would have fitted on one postage stamp. The card featured an image of a Christmas tree etched on a tiny piece of glass.

Why do people open Advent calendars in the run up to Christmas?

The period of four weeks leading up to Christmas is called Advent, from the Latin *adveneo* meaning 'to come'. In this context it refers to the coming of Jesus, and so in the Christian Church has always been a time of preparation, in expectation of the Feast of the Nativity.

In many households the days left until Christmas are counted down with the aid of an Advent calendar. From 1 December onwards, one numbered door or window is opened to reveal the image – and now, more often than not, the chocolate or toy – hidden behind it. It used to be the case that the last window was for the 24 December, which had an image of the Nativity behind it, but now calendars can last as far as the New Year!

It is easy to see how the season of Advent came about in the early Church but what of the calendars used to count down the days to Christmas?

The first Advent calendars, as we would recognise them, were made in the middle of the nineteenth century. Even before that, however, German Lutherans were already marking off the days of Advent by some physical means, as they had done since at least the beginning of the century. In some households this meant lighting a new candle each day or hanging up a religious image, but could be something as simple (and cost-free) as marking a line in chalk on the door of the house. If candles were used, they were mounted on a device called an Advent clock.

The first recognisable Advent calendar, however, didn't appear until 1851, and even then it was a handmade creation. There is some debate as to when the first printed calendar appeared. Some say that it was produced in 1902 or 1903, in Hamburg, Germany; others claim that it did not appear until 1908, and that it was the creation of one Gerhard Lang, a printer from Munich.

Lang's calendar was certainly the basis of our modern Advent calendars. His first efforts were made up of 24 tiny coloured pictures that had to be stuck onto a piece of cardboard. In the years to come, however, he was to introduce the doors that are so integral to Advent calendars today.

During the Second World War, the manufacture of Advent calendars ceased, as cardboard was rationed. However, once the war was over, the firm of Richard Sellmer Verlag began producing them once more, and was almost wholly responsible for their widespread popularity.

Although it might seem like a more recent addition, Advent calendars replete with chocolate treats have actually been around for at least half a century, and were certainly available by 1958.

Advent calendars are no longer only made of card either. Cloth versions, with pockets in place of doors to open, are popular, as are strings of stockings which have to be filled with toys and gifts for the child by a benevolent parent. And then there are the true twenty-first century Advent calendars that can be 'opened' and viewed online.

However, in Germany, the spiritual home of the Advent calendar, certain towns go that extra mile. The *Rathaus* of Gengenbach, a town located within Germany's Black Forest, is turned into a gigantic Advent calendar every year, thanks to the fact that it conveniently has 24 main windows. Starting on the evening of 30 November, each of these windows is unveiled in turn to reveal a festive scene.

In the town of Reith, each of the 24 windows is actually located in a different building and is referred to as the town's walking Advent calendar, while in Dresden the city's Advent calendar is constructed at the site of its Christmas market, in the *Striezelmarkt*, in the form of a fairytale castle.

—— The A to Z of Christmas ——

is for December

December was the tenth month of the Roman calendar (*decem* meaning 'ten' in Latin). The Anglo-Saxons referred to it as both *Winter Monath* and *Yule Monath*, but after many of them were converted to Christianity it became known as *Heligh Monath* or 'holy month'.

1 December itself is the feast day of Saint Eligius – the patron saint of goldsmiths and other metalworkers, including blacksmiths – who died on this day AD 660. There are a number of legends which are often linked to Saint Dunstan (another smithying saint), but which have also been applied to Saint Eligius.

In one, the Saint, formerly a blacksmith himself, was working at his forge when the Devil paid him a visit. The Devil had disguised himself as a beautiful woman, with a view to leading his victim astray. However, the Saint spotted Satan's cloven hooves poking out from beneath the woman's dress, and grabbed the Devil's nose with his red hot pincers, thus foiling the Evil One's diabolical scheme.

According to another legend, Satan returned again as a weary traveller in need of a horseshoe. The Saint saw through the disguise a second time and beat the Devil until he pleaded for mercy, and swore never to enter any house with a horseshoe above the door.

Why are stockings hung up on Christmas Eve?

It has long been the practice that on Christmas Eve, children (and sometimes optimistic adults) hang stockings by the fire, or at the foot of their bed, in the hope that Father Christmas will deposit presents for them to open on Christmas morning. Nowadays, of course, pillow cases have become a popular alternative.

In Clement Clarke Moore's popular poem, 'An Account of a Visit from Saint Nicholas' we are told that:

> The stockings were hung by the chimney with care,
>
> In the hope that St Nicholas would soon be there...

And indeed, this tradition has its origins in one of the myths surrounding the original Santa Claus himself, Saint Nicholas.

The legend can be traced back to the eighth century and involves a father and his three daughters. This family had fallen on hard times and could no longer afford even the basics, such as food and clothing. There was certainly no way that the poor man could afford the dowries that the girls would need to get married. Faced with such a dire predicament the girls' father decided that the only option left open to them, to save them from starvation, was for the girls to enter into the world's oldest profession.

One night, however, Saint Nicholas happened to be passing the house where the family lived and he heard the father and his daughters bemoaning their desperate situation. Nicholas had been left a considerable fortune by his parents, but now there were only three bags of gold left. No matter – it was enough to help the distraught spinsters.

Having collected the cash from his home, Nicholas returned later that night. One by one he dropped the bags of gold down the chimney where they landed in the girls' stockings that had been hung up to dry in front of the fire. And so, the daughters were saved from a life of iniquity and poverty.

In some versions of the story Nicholas threw the bags of gold in through a window, as each of the girls came of marriageable age, and in others the gold drops down the chimney to land in the girls' shoes, rather than their stockings. But the sentiment is the same in all of them, with Saint Nicholas cast in the role of the generous, yet secretive, benefactor.

Although it is difficult to determine when the practice of hanging up stockings specifically to receive presents from Saint Nicholas began, we do know that it was so popular by the early seventeenth century that one Protestant priest complained about parents telling their children that Saint Nicholas had brought them their presents, as it was, 'a bad custom, because it points children to the saint, while yet we know that not Saint Nicholas but the holy Christ Child gives us all good things for body and soul…'

The three bags of gold with which the saint saved the poor girls' reputations has survived to this day in another, rather more surprising form. A symbol of giving, the three bags of gold have become the three balls on the traditional pawnbroker's sign. This dates from the Middle Ages, and Lombard Street in London. At this time, the area became home to many pawnbrokers who, when searching for a symbol to represent their trade, had to look no further than the Church of Saint Nicholas, which stood in Lombard Street itself. The statue of the saint on top of the church was shown holding the familiar money bags, which

Medieval artists had painted as being round, and so appeared as balls. This symbol of the three bags of gold was then adopted by the pawnbrokers' businesses and has remained associated with them ever since.

As a consequence, the hanging out of stockings on Christmas Eve is one of the older traditions that have become linked to the modern commercial Christmas. Nowadays many people seem to have forgotten that once upon a time Santa only delivered presents to those deserving of such generosity as a result of their own good behaviour during the previous year.

It is traditional among many families for each child to receive a tangerine in their stocking, along with all their other presents. One of the oldest varieties is the Dancy tangerine, which has a loose, pliable peel. The tangerine used to be considered an exotic fruit and, as it was only available in December, it made the perfect Christmas treat for children to receive from Father Christmas. There is also a legend that the tradition was started by twelfth century French nuns who left socks full of fruit, nuts *and tangerines* at the houses of the poor!

—— The A to Z of Christmas ——

is for Ebenezer Scrooge

Ebenezer Scrooge is the protagonist of Charles Dickens' famous festive fable, *A Christmas Carol*. A miserable miser at the beginning of the book, he is shown the error of his money-grubbing ways by three spirits – the ghosts of Christmas Past, Christmas

Present and Christmas Yet to Come. By the end of the tale he has made amends and shows particular generosity to his employee Bob Cratchit and his family.

Popular in the eighteenth and nineteenth centuries, the name Ebenezer (sometimes spelled 'Ebenezar') is Hebrew in origin and means 'stone of the help'. It is possible that Dickens took the miser's surname from the now obscure English verb 'scrouge', meaning 'squeeze' or 'press', although various other sources of inspiration have been suggested. These include Jemmy Wood, the owner of the Gloucester Old Bank and possibly Britain's first millionaire, a noted eighteenth century eccentric and miser by the name of John Elwes, and one Ebeneezer Scroggie, the Scotsman who won the catering contract for the King George IV's 1822 visit to Scotland, during which the king wore a highland outfit of bright red Royal Tartan and pink tights!

Dickens more or less invented the Christmas spirit, goodwill to all men and general jollity, in this classic ghost story, which also gave us such memorable characters as Tiny Tim and Bob Cratchit. Dickens himself wrote in the preface to the novella, "I have endeavoured in this Ghostly little book, to raise the Ghost of an Idea, which shall not put my readers out of humour with themselves, with each other, with the season, or with me. May it haunt their houses pleasantly, and no one wish to lay it. Their faithful Friend and Servant, C. D." But *A Christmas Carol* wasn't the only festive-themed story penned by Charles Dickens. His other Christmas Books include *The Chimes* (1844), *The*

Cricket on the Hearth (1845), *The Battle of Life* (1846) and
The Haunted Man and the Ghost's Bargain (1848).

Did you know...?

The Men Who Will Not Be Blamed For
Nothing, a Steampunk band from London,
produced their own very particular take
on the story as part of their special limited
edition 7" A Very Steampunk Christmas
EP, released in December 2010. Ebenezer's
Carol casts Scrooge as a money-lender and
Bob Cratchit as his thuggish debt collector,
who hires Dickens (his ghostwriter, if you
like) to put a twist on his tale to make him
more popular with the masses.

For a book that took only six weeks to write in 1843,
A Christmas Carol has enjoyed an enduring popularity
with the British public, and the wider world beyond.
There have been countless adaptations for stage and

screen, including the Bill Murray vehicle *Scrooged* (1988), *The Muppet Christmas Carol* (1992), and Robert Zameckis's 3D CGI performance capture movie starring Jim Carrey as not just Ebenezer Scrooge, but also all three ghosts. There have even been radio plays, operatic versions, graphic novels and many parodies (such as *Blackadder's Christmas Carol*, produced by the BBC in 1988).

Incredibly, a replica tombstone made for the 1984 US TV movie adaptation starring George C. Scott (for which he was nominated for an Emmy), is still in situ in the churchyard of St Chad's Church in Shrewsbury, Shropshire.

Why is 26 December called Boxing Day?

It has nothing to do with the sport of boxing, if that's what you're wondering. Boxing Day has been known by that name since the Middle Ages because of its connection to alms boxes.

It was on this day that alms boxes – the boxes placed in churches to collect money for the needy – would be opened by the priests and the money, given by the better-off parishioners, distributed to the poor of the parish. This was once known as the 'dole of the Christmas box'. It led, in time, to the practice of giving those who had provided a service over the previous year – such as delivering your milk or mail – a seasonal thank-you in the form of a 'Christmas box', hence, Boxing Day.

This type of collecting box was first brought to Britain by the Romans, but rather than distribute the money to the poor, the Romans used it to pay for the games which took place during the winter celebrations.

After the sixteenth century it was common practice for apprentices and household servants to ask their masters (and even their masters' customers) for money at Christmas time. Any gifts of money they received were placed inside an earthenware 'box' – which looked more like a piggy bank, complete with a slit in the top – which was then broken open on 26 December.

By the late-eighteenth century, wealthy landowners would box up any food left over from the Christmas Day celebrations, sometimes adding other gifts as well, and distribute them the day after to their tenants. Interestingly, if Christmas Day fell on a Saturday, then Boxing Day would be passed over to the Monday, rather than taking place on the Sunday straight after Christmas.

The Boxing Day fox hunt was once another well-known tradition, until hunting with dogs was banned in England and Wales in 2005. This practice takes us back to the saint whose feast day falls on 26 December, Saint Stephen, or rather a confusion over saints with the same name.

Saint Stephen was the first Christian martyr, having been stoned to death for preaching about Jesus in AD 33, not long after Christ's crucifixion. Saint Stephen is now the patron of deacons and invoked by those suffering from headaches (possibly a connection with him having been stoned). He is also the protector of builders and bricklayers.

Saint Stephen of Sweden, on the other hand, lived in the ninth century. He is the patron saint of horses thanks to the manner of his death. Swedish Steve owned five horses, which allowed him to travel great distances in his efforts to convert the people of Scandinavia. On one such missionary journey, when he was riding through a forest, he was attacked by robbers who killed him and stole his horses. His murderers lashed his corpse to the back of a wild colt, hoping that the animal would carry Stephen's body far from the scene of the crime, and so help them to get away with murder. However, according to the legend, this particular horse did not bolt and instead calmly carried Stephen back to his home in Norrtalje. As a result, the robbers were apprehended and put to death for their crimes. Stephen's grave subsequently became a holy site for horses!

However, over time, the two Stephens have become muddled in people's minds so that the first Christian martyr's feast day has become associated with those things actually special to the Swedish saint. This, in turn, has resulted in some peculiar, equine-related Boxing Day traditions.

In the past, in Germany, horsemen would ride their steeds around *inside* the church during the Saint Stephen's Day service. In both Austria and England, horses were bled (having been ridden until they had worked up a sweat) to ensure the animals' good health for the year ahead, by supposedly letting out the evil spirits living in the horse.

Boxing Day has always been a time for families to get together and take some exercise. As well as going for pleasant country walks, it is traditional for people to partake of various sporting activities on this day, such as ice skating and horseracing, or at least enjoy them as spectators. In Medieval times, Boxing Day was a traditional time for mummers to perform their plays and sword dances.

Another curious Christmas, or rather Boxing Day, custom, the Hunting of the Wren, also connects back to the first Christian martyr. One legend recounts how, having been imprisoned for preaching about Christ, Stephen was on the verge of escaping his captors when chirruping wrens woke the jailers and, as a result, Stephen's escape attempt was foiled.

Did you know...?

The actual practice of the Hunting of the Wren may pre-date even Christianity coming to the British Isles, as the shamanic druids of the Celtic peoples captured wrens for use in prophecy.

The day after Christmas, the descendants of the Celts would go out to hunt and kill a wren. Once the little bird was dead – usually having been stoned to death, suffering the same fate as Saint Stephen as punishment – it would be fastened to the top of a pole, wings outstretched, decorated with ribbons and sprigs of holy, and then paraded from house to house, while the 'Wren boys', their faces blackened by burnt cork, chanted:

> *We hunted the wren for Robin the Bobbin,*
>
> *We hunted the wren for Jack of the Can,*
>
> *We hunted the wren for Robin the Bobbin,*
>
> *We hunted the wren for everyone.*

At each house, the wren-hunters would collect offerings of money or food.

On the Isle of Man, when as many offerings had been collected as possible, the ritual came to an end with the wren being carried to the parish churchyard where it was promptly buried with all due reverence. The funeral over, everyone present would leave the churchyard, form a circle and start dancing.

It was normally considered unlucky to kill or even harm a wren, apart from during the season of peace and goodwill (towards one's fellow man – but not wrens, obviously). Those who made an offering to the begging wren-bearers would receive one of the tiny bird's feathers in return for good luck, as they were supposed to avert shipwreck. Because of its association with this tiniest of British birds, 26 December is also sometimes known as Wren Day.

The practice was still being carried out in Ireland in the 1920s, although the rhyme recited in that country was a little different.

The wren, the wren, the king of all birds,

Saint Stephen's Day was caught in the furze;

Although he is little, his family's great,

I pray you, good landlady, give us a treat.

What is figgy pudding?

Let's get one thing clear from the start; figgy pudding is not Christmas pudding. That's plum pudding. The constituent ingredient of figgy pudding is figs, whereas plum pudding – the traditional Christmas pudding – should be made with plums. Easy, isn't it? So, in that case, why is everyone so familiar with figgy pudding when hardly anybody eats it anymore?

Well, it's all down to the carol 'We Wish You a Merry Christmas' in which the name of the pudding is mentioned:

Oh, bring us a figgy pudding;

Oh, bring us a figgy pudding;

Oh, bring us a figgy pudding and a cup of good cheer.

We won't go until we get some;

We won't go until we get some;

We won't go until we get some, so bring some out here.

Many people would be surprised by the appearance of figgy pudding, which looks like a white Christmas pudding. The following recipe for Figgy Pudding serves four.

Figgy Pudding

280 ml/½ pt of milk

200 g/8 oz flour

175 g/6 oz dried figs

140 ml/¼ pt of brandy

100 g/4 oz suet

100 g/4 oz prunes

75 g/3 oz raisins (or sultanas)

50 g/2 oz dried apricots

50 g/2 oz dates

25 g/1 oz dried apples

1 tbs of honey

½ tsp grated lemon peel

½ tsp of ground cinnamon

¼ tsp of ground nutmeg

¼ tsp of ginger

Whipped cream

This dish needs a little preparation time. The day before you plan to make the figgy pudding, soak the prunes, apricots and apples in water, and soak the raisins (or sultanas) in the brandy. Then before you prepare the dish, remove the stones from the prunes and the figs.

Now we come to the making of the pudding itself. Sift the flour into a mixing bowl, stir in the suet and mix together with cold water until a soft dough is formed. Turn the dough out onto a floured board and knead it until smooth. Grease a large pudding basin and roll out two-thirds of the pastry to line it.

Melt the honey and stir in the grated lemon peel, cinnamon, nutmeg and ginger, before adding this to the soaked fruits and brandy mixture. Mix well and then place inside the pastry-lined bowl. Moisten the edges of the pastry with water and cover with a lid rolled out from the rest of the pastry. Press the edges together to seal it. Cover the lot with greased greaseproof paper (or aluminium foil) and steam for two hours, topping up the boiling water from time to time to ensure that it doesn't evaporate. To serve, turn out onto a plate and serve with the whipped cream.

Today's traditional Christmas pudding, like so much of our modern Christmas, comes from the Victorian era. However, long before anyone ate Christmas pudding of any description, people living during the Medieval period would have tucked into a hearty bowl of frumenty – that's a spicy porridge-like dish made with almond milk, to you and me. The following recipe dates from the fifteenth century.

Frumenty

250 g/10 oz cracked wheat

5 cups of water

⅓ cup of beef stock

⅓ cup of almond milk

2 beaten egg yolks

A pinch of dried saffron threads

A pinch of salt

Boil the wheat in the water until its softened (which should take about 15 minutes) and then remove it from the heat, leaving it to stand so that the remaining water is absorbed. Add the beef stock and the almond milk, and bring it back to the boil, before reducing the heat to a low setting. Stir the mixture for approximately 5 minutes. Stir in the beaten egg yolks and saffron, and keep stirring until the egg starts to thicken. It is important not to let the mixture boil. Take it off the heat and let it stand for another 5 minutes (during which time the mixture will continue to thicken) before serving.

If you don't want to go to the trouble of making almond milk you can simply substitute it with ordinary milk. But if you do fancy the idea of making almond milk for yourself, here's how to do it.

Almond milk

100 g/4 oz blanched almonds
1–2 tbs of ice water
1 cup of boiling water

Grind the almonds with the ice water in a mortar (or put them in a blender). Put the resulting paste into a bowl, adding the boiling water. Allow the mixture to stand for 15 minutes before straining it through a metal sieve. The resulting almond milk will last for three days if kept refrigerated.

Frumenty was eaten as an accompaniment to meat, traditionally venison, and was also served up with porpoise! As well as being a popular part of the traditional Celtic Christmas meal, it was also eaten on Mothering Sunday, when the inclusion of eggs would have provided a brief respite from the traditional Lenten fast. Although the idea of eating porridge on Christmas day might seem a little strange to us now, in areas of Scandinavia it's still part of Christmas dinner.

By Tudor times, people had graduated from eating spiced porridge, to consuming Christmas puddings which – rather like mince pies – contained more than just the dried fruit and spices we're familiar with today. A typical Tudor pudding would contain meat as well as oatmeal and spices. The preferred method of cooking this little lot was to boil it, and to stop the pudding falling apart in the bubbling vat it was stuffed into a pig's intestine first, rather like sausages are today. In fact the pudding ended up looking like a fat sausage and would be served by the slice. But another hundred years later and the list of ingredients had changed again.

If one recipe for Christmas pudding can be considered more traditional than any other, then it is probably that enjoyed by the Pudding King himself, George I.

King George I's Christmas Pudding (1714)

10 eggs
680 g/1½ lb shredded suet
450 g/1 lb dried plums
450 g/1 lb raisins
450 g/1 lb mixed peel
450 g/1 lb currants
450 g/1 lb sultanas
450 g/1 lb flour
450 g/1 lb sugar

450 g/1 lb breadcrumbs

1 tsp mixed spice

1 tsp grated nutmeg

280 ml/½ pt of milk

½ tsp of salt

The juice of a lemon

A large glass of brandy

Having mixed up all of the ingredients let the whole lot stand for 12 hours before boiling the mixture for 8 hours. Come Christmas Day you boil it again for 2 hours. This list of ingredients above will produce about 9 lbs of pudding.

An alternative recipe for a rather more alcoholic plum pudding comes from the Edwardians, who are known for being just as wildly excessive as people are today.

Plum Pudding (1909)

1 kg/2¼ lbs raisins

1 kg/2¼ lbs currants

175 g/6 oz finely chopped candied peel

13 eggs

850 ml/1½ pt of milk

1½ cups of breadcrumbs
680 g/1½ lbs flour
680 g/1½ lbs finely chopped suet
3 wineglasses of brandy
2 wineglasses of rum

Mix the ingredients together well and then spread between two buttered basins, to make two large puddings. Boil them for 14 hours.

Halfway between frumenty and plum pudding is a concoction called plum porridge. Plum porridge was made with meat broth, thickened with breadcrumbs, and then flavoured by adding the dried fruit which gave it its name: dried plums (so, in other words prunes), raisins, currants, sugar, ginger, other spices and even wine. It was also served at the beginning of the Christmas meal, rather than the end.

During the eighteenth century this porridge became thicker and was boiled in a cloth. By the nineteenth century the meat component had gone completely and the dish was served as a dessert, doused in flaming brandy with a sprig of holly in the top.

It was during the Victorians' reinvention of Christmas that plum pudding found its place as a highlight of the Christmas meal. That renowned writer and re-inventor of Christmas, Charles Dickens, wrote about its importance and grandeur in *A Christmas Carol*:

> ... like a speckled cannon-ball, so hard and firm, blazing in half a quarter of ignited brandy, and bedecked with Christmas holly

stuck into the top. Oh, a wonderful pudding!
Bob Cratchit said, and calmly too, that he
regarded it as the greatest success achieved by
Mrs Cratchit since their wedding.

When Queen Victoria was on the throne, the British travelled to all corners of the globe, taking their traditions and customs with them. So the Christmas pudding travelled around the world too, becoming an intrinsic part of Christmas meals enjoyed by ex-pats living in Australia and British troops fighting in the Crimea. Even the poorhouses provided some manner of plum pudding for those incarcerated within on Christmas Day.

The traditional time to prepare the pudding to be eaten on Christmas Day was the last Sunday before Advent, called Stir-up Sunday. Each member of the family was supposed to take a turn at stirring the mixture, and make a wish whilst doing so.

But why was it called Stir-up Sunday? That might sound like a silly question now, but the name has nothing to do with people stirring Christmas pudding mixture. It actually comes from a passage in the Prayer Book related to Saint Andrew's Day:

Stir up, we beseech Thee, O Lord, the will
of thy faithful people.

Stir-up Sunday is usually also the one closest to Saint Andrew's Day, 30 November, and perhaps it is because of this instruction from the Prayer Book that people have for so many years made their Christmas puddings on that particular day.

Of course brandy butter is as traditional as the

Christmas pudding it usually accompanies and if you fancy making it yourself this year, you can't go wrong with this simple recipe.

Brandy Butter

100 g/4 oz butter

50 g/2 oz icing sugar

1 tbs brandy

Cream the sugar and butter together, stir in the brandy and then beat into the mix. Refrigerate until it's needed. And that's it!

The A to Z of Christmas

is for Fairy

When somebody finishes decorating a Christmas tree, they usually top it off with a fairy or a star. But why should a fairy feature on the tree? And why a star for that matter?

The star is probably easier to explain – it is supposed to represent the Christmas star that led the wise men (and others) to the place of Christ's birth. And the fairy is there for much the same reason, only it isn't supposed to be a fairy – it's supposed to be an angel, and is meant to make people think of the angel who brought glad tidings of great joy to the shepherds out in the fields, keeping watch over their flock by night.

The traditional Christmas pantomime is partly to blame for the confusion, the winged figure at the top of the tree becoming entangled with the good fairy who is so often present in pantomime productions.

In times past, the figure at the top of the tree was the baby Jesus himself, but in late seventeenth Germany, Jesus became a shining angel instead. Of course, there is another story as to how the fairy came to be sitting on top of the Christmas tree.

Father Christmas was having a very bad day; there was simply so much to do in preparation for Christmas Eve but there just weren't enough hours in the day. The elves were trying to be helpful, but everything they did only seemed to worsen Father Christmas's mood. In the end, one of the elves suggested calling on a few fairy friends to come and help out, hoping that their gentle spirits would soothe Santa's increasingly frazzled nerves. A few of them gathered round and started helping out but although it made the elves feel better, it did nothing to alleviate Father Christmas's bad mood. The bravest of the little fairies got hold of a Christmas tree and asked Father Christmas very sweetly where she should put it, to which he replied, "For all I care, you can shove it up your..." (You can probably work out the rest for yourself.)

Why do people put up Christmas decorations?

People have always festooned their homes with some manner of decorations, whether boughs of winter greenery or with enough electric lights to double their energy bills for the year. But where did it all start?

Our Norse ancestors used evergreens – mainly holly, ivy, mistletoe and the branches of fir trees – to decorate their homes during the winter months, to remind people that life would return to the world again.

In time, other man-made decorations, such as bows of red ribbon and lit candles would be added to enhance what nature had already provided.

With the growth of towns and cities, by the late-nineteenth century, it was not so easy for some people to simply take a stroll through the nearest stretch of woodland to collect their winter greenery and so it was that commercialism played its hand; someone had to bring to market for the urban masses what had once been free to all.

This is the case now, of course, more than ever before. Much of the mistletoe that goes into decorating our homes at Christmas time, for example, is actually harvested from apple orchards in France.

Following the example set by Queen Victoria and Prince Albert in the 1840s, the trend of having a

Christmas tree in the home grew during the nineteenth century, and so the demand increased to have things to put on it.

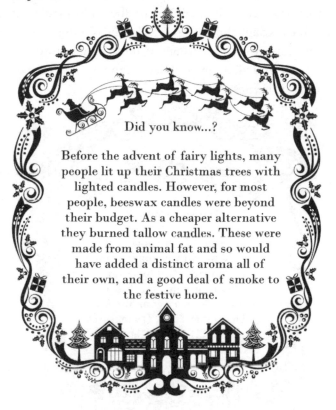

Did you know...?

Before the advent of fairy lights, many people lit up their Christmas trees with lighted candles. However, for most people, beeswax candles were beyond their budget. As a cheaper alternative they burned tallow candles. These were made from animal fat and so would have added a distinct aroma all of their own, and a good deal of smoke to the festive home.

Other than the lit candles, of one form or another, at first many Christmas tree decorations were of an edible nature. There were sweets, fruit and even wafers; then came small presents and paper ornaments. By the

1880s glass ornaments were all the rage, with baubles replacing the once traditional apples hung on the old-fashioned Paradise tree (a precursor to the modern Christmas tree) – a reminder of the forbidden fruit tasted by Adam and Eve in the Garden of Eden.

And now we have strings of fairy lights, tinsel by the metre and all manner of decorations with which to adorn our homes.

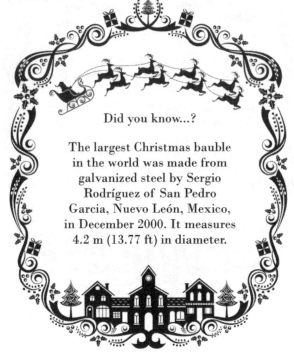

Did you know...?

The largest Christmas bauble in the world was made from galvanized steel by Sergio Rodríguez of San Pedro Garcia, Nuevo León, Mexico, in December 2000. It measures 4.2 m (13.77 ft) in diameter.

There is a popular belief that it is unlucky to leave Christmas decorations up after Twelfth Night. But why should this be the case?

Druidic beliefs held that wood spirits were in the evergreens brought into the home, and that they could cause mischief in the household. However, they were prevented from doing so during the period lasting from Christmas Eve to Twelfth Night. After that they were free to do their worst again.

Long after the original pagan rituals and traditions had been replaced or amalgamated with Christian-flavoured versions, in the Middle Ages people found it hard to shake off their devotedly held superstitious beliefs so easily. Common folklore still said that the leafy boughs brought into the home at Christmastide were verily budding with nature spirits which could cause mischief if they weren't handled properly.

And the superstition has lasted to this day, even though the reasons for this have in most cases long been forgotten.

If you fancy making some of your own edible tree decorations, as your forebears once did, why not try this recipe for cinnamon and ginger biscuits?

Cinnamon and Ginger Biscuit Decorations

100 g/4 oz caster sugar
100 g/4 oz unsalted butter
200 g/8 oz plain flour, sifted

1 tsp of ground ginger

½ tsp of cinnamon

½ tsp of vanilla extract

1 small egg, beaten

Thin red ribbon or gold cord

To make the biscuits, start by creaming the sugar and butter together in a bowl, then add the egg. Sift the flour into the bowl and stir it in along with the cinnamon and ginger. Add the vanilla extract. Mix all of this together until a firm dough is produced. Ideally you want to leave the dough in the fridge for 1–2 hours at this point, but you can get away without doing so if time's not on your side.

Roll the dough out flat, and fairly thin, before cutting it into the shapes you desire. There are plenty of seasonal biscuit cutters that are ideal for this job. Just remember, the less complicated the shape, the less likely it is to crumble and break, and so will survive the ultimate transition to your Christmas tree. Pierce the unbaked biscuit with a knitting needle or skewer to make a hole through which to thread the ribbon later.

Grease and flour a baking sheet and preheat the oven to 190°C. Place the biscuit shapes onto the sheet and cook at the top of the oven for 10 minutes. Once they're done, leave them on the baking sheet for a few minutes before transferring them to a wire rack to finish cooling.

Thread a length of the ribbon or cord through the hole in each biscuit and tie it to form a loop, so you can hang them up. If you want, you can decorate the biscuit decorations before hanging them on your tree; you could use white icing or melted chocolate and then embellish your miniature masterpieces with silver balls, hundreds and thousands, or chopped nuts and glacé cherries.

And you're done. Just don't expect these decorations to last until Twelfth Night, or even Boxing Day for that matter!

Did you know...?

In the United States, it is not uncommon for people to adorn their trees with their own edible decorations, normally pretzels and popcorn. The pretzels are often combined to create amazing shapes, while the popcorn is made into long strings before being draped on the tree.

is for Glastonbury Thorn

The Glastonbury Thorn is a hawthorn, of a type that originates in the Middle East, but which specifically grows in the grounds of Glastonbury Abbey in Somerset, England. Legend has it that it grew from where Joseph of Arimathea – Jesus's uncle – laid his staff, and the plant has flowered every Christmas Day since.

A cutting from the Glastonbury Thorn was sent to the monarch each Christmas by the Vicar and Mayor of Glastonbury. However, the tree was pronounced dead in June 1991, and cut down the following February. Fortunately, plenty of cuttings were taken from the plant before its destruction so that a new Thorn could be planted. In fact, the hawthorn growing in the grounds of Glastonbury Abbey before 1991 was itself supposedly a cutting from the original staff-born shrub, planted in secret after the former was destroyed.

Only hawthorn trees that budded or were grafted from the original exist. The plants actually blossom twice a year, in May as well as at Christmas. The blossoms of the Christmas shoots are smaller than the ones the plant produces in May and do not produce any haws, the small, oval, berry-like fruit of the hawthorn, which are dark red in colour.

Where does the Christmas wreath come from?

To the pagan peoples of Europe, evergreens possessed magical powers; how else was it that the holly, fir and ivy stayed green and kept their leaves in the depths of winter when other plants vanished and trees were left as leafless skeletons compared to the green glory of summer?

Some of these seemingly magical plants even produced fruit and flowers throughout the winter months. What other possible explanation could there be? So, understandably, in the freezing depths of winter when all other life seemed to have disappeared from the world, these same pagan peoples brought evergreens into their homes, partly to pay homage to their gods – who kept life going throughout these dark days – and partly in the hope that some of the plants' magical protection might rub off on them.

Our Roman ancestors also considered evergreens lucky and during the feast of Saturnalia, (which took place around what is now Christmas time) they too decorated their homes with boughs of holly and the like. They were also fans of the laurel, which was supposed to have the power to protect and purify. Of course it also stood as a symbol of victory and honour and was used to decorate those who had achieved some form of distinction in Ancient Rome. (It is from this tradition that we get the expression 'resting on your laurels'.)

Thanks to their connections with the concept of eternal life, it is easy to see how evergreens came to be such a central part of the Christian feast of Christmas. After all, the Church teaches that Jesus rose from the dead to eternal life himself, and offers the same to his faithful servants.

There were also other, more immediate benefits to bringing evergreens inside. Pine branches gave the home a fresh, clean smell, and pine-scented air fresheners and sprays are still a popular choice today – particularly for the bathroom. Rosemary, the herb of remembrance (as mentioned by Ophelia in a scene from Shakespeare's *Hamlet*), added its own fragrant aroma. It was particularly appropriate as Christmas is also that time of year when people remember friends and family, as well as the birth of Jesus.

The presence of evergreen plants in the home during the festive season has lived on in several forms; through the Christmas tree, in carols such as 'The Holly and the Ivy' and 'Deck the Halls', and of course with the Christmas wreath.

Other evergreen rings were also transformed into symbols of the Christian Church. Branches of evergreens were twisted around a hoop which was then hung up. Candles were attached to the outer edge of the ring. When lit, and with the ring having been spun, the candle flames created a whirling circle of light. Pagan peoples believed that this magical symbol would banish the winter darkness, helping to hasten the lengthening days and new life that came with the spring.

This evergreen ring subsequently became the Advent ring that appears in churches four Sundays before Christmas. One candle is lit each Sunday with a fifth candle at the centre of the ring being lit on Christmas Day.

How to make a Christmas wreath

1. First of all make yourself a circular metal frame. This could be something as simple as a coat hanger bent out of shape.
2. Using wire or garden twine (or just plain old string) to hold it in place, cover the ring with sphagnum moss (which you can acquire from a florist's).
3. Add green foliage to the ring, using plants like holly, ivy and swathes of an evergreen, like fir.
4. Push stems of berries through the moss to add some colour.
5. If you want you can even add some seasonal flowers, such as Christmas roses.

Tie a loop of string to the back of the wreath or attach another piece of wire, so that you can hang it from your front door. And there you have it; one Christmas wreath.

MERRY CHRISTMAS

Did you know...?

The vibrantly coloured Poinsettia, with its bright red leaves, that has become such a Christmas institution is named after the first American ambassador to Mexico, Dr Joel Roberts Poinsett. In Mexico the plant goes by the name of the Flower of the Holy Night, but when Poinsett brought it back to America is was renamed in his honour.

In Mexico, the plant has legendary origins that are associated with Christmas. It was once the tradition in that country to place gifts for Jesus on church altars on Christmas Eve. One poor boy had nothing to give and, in his distress, knelt outside the church window and prayed. And there, where he had been kneeling, a beautiful plant with red leaves sprang up.

The town of Encinitas in California is known as the Poinsettia capital of the world because of the profusion of plants found there.

Why are mince pies eaten at Christmas time?

Before we answer that particular seasonal question, we should really start by asking ourselves 'What is a mince pie?' After all, the mince pies we enjoy at Christmas are very different from those eaten hundreds of years ago, when they first became popular. Firstly, they had a different name, secondly, they were a different size and shape, and thirdly, they had some very different ingredients.

Following the Crusades of the twelfth and thirteenth centuries, knights and their followers returned from the Holy Land bearing new and exciting spices. The tradition then began of baking a pie to celebrate Christ's birthday. A vital step in producing this masterpiece was the addition of three spices brought back from Christ's native land. These were cinnamon, cloves and nutmeg and they represented the three gifts given to the Christ child by the Magi. Later, during the Medieval period, gold itself was used in the gilded decoration of the pie – for those that could afford such extravagance!

As well as having a symbolic significance, the spices would have also helped to hide the taste of any slightly 'off' meat that might have made it into the pie filling. For as well as being made with a mixture of dried fruit and spices, cooks also added all manner of shredded meat as well – whatever was available to them at the time – such as goose and veal, hence the filling being referred to as 'mincemeat'.

91

The origins of the mince pie can also be traced back to the 'chewette', a Medieval pastry, which contained liver or other chopped meat, mixed in with boiled eggs and ginger, and which was then either baked or fried. Just for variety, the chewette's filling would sometimes be replaced with dried fruit and other sweet ingredients.

During the Middle Ages, it was the custom to bake a large mince pie for Christmas that could be enjoyed by the whole family – not dozens of smaller ones as we do now. In some parts of England, these 'Christmas Pies' were known as 'coffins', due to them being rectangular in shape. By the sixteenth century, at the time of the Tudor monarchy, the eating of mince pies had already become a regular part of the Christmas festivities, but now they were often oval, shaped to look like the Christ child's cradle and called 'Crib pies'. By the 1600s they could even come adorned with a pastry Baby Jesus!

Included in the list of ingredients for a mince pie recipe from the early seventeenth century are:

two rabbits

two pigeons

two partridges

a hare

a pheasant

a capon

the livers of all these animals

eggs

pickled mushrooms

dried fruit

spices

A monster pie, like this one, could weigh anything up to 100 kg (or 220 lb), and had to be held together with iron clamps for it to be baked successfully.

If you fancy having a go at creating your own Medieval Christmas Pie, then why not try out this recipe?

Christmas Pie

450 g/1 lb plain flour

200 g/8 oz suet

Pinch of salt

200 g/8 oz mixed meat (beef, pork and lamb work well)

1 onion, chopped

1 carrot, chopped

2 cloves of garlic

2 tbs mixed fruit

2 tbs brown sugar

2 tbs red wine

1 tbs coriander, chopped

1 tbs ginger, chopped

2 tsps thyme, chopped

1½ tsps cumin

1½ tsps cinnamon

Salt and pepper

1 lemon

1 egg

Cover the suet with water in a pan and boil. Take off the heat; add the flour and salt and mix well to form a dough. When it is cool enough to handle, roll the dough out. Grease and flour a shallow dish and line it with the pastry you have made, keeping some back to make a lid.

To make the filling, mix together the minced meats, adding the coriander, ginger and garlic, and the zest of the lemon. Mix together the sugar, cumin, cinnamon, salt and pepper.

Now to make the pie itself. Layer the ingredients into the pie dish, starting with the meat mixture, then the mixed fruit, chopped vegetables, and the sugar mixture sprinkled on top. Wetting the edges of the pastry with water, place the lid you have made from the rest of the dough on top. Make a hole in the top of the pie and brush the lid with beaten egg.

Bake the pie in a pre-heated oven at 220°C for 20–25 minutes, or until golden brown. Your Christmas Pie is best served warm.

Following the English Civil War and the overthrow of the monarchy, mince pies were just one of many festive traditions to be banned by Oliver Cromwell's Puritan parliament. But they weren't forgotten by those who had enjoyed them for so long. They lost the tag of Christmas pie, becoming known simply as 'minced' or 'shredded' pies. They also became smaller and round in shape, and so survived the Puritans' attempts to stamp them out altogether, along with all the other trappings of Christmas.

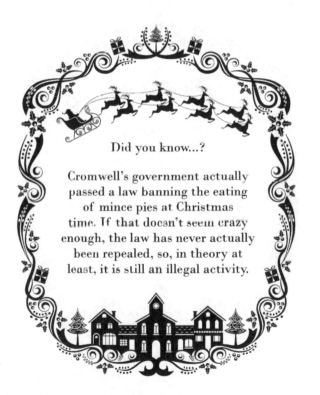

Did you know...?

Cromwell's government actually passed a law banning the eating of mince pies at Christmas time. If that doesn't seem crazy enough, the law has never actually been repealed, so, in theory at least, it is still an illegal activity.

When the monarchy was restored in 1660, Christmas was restored along with it. But the mince pie remained the small, circular, humble thing that it had become during the time of the Commonwealth, just like those that we still enjoy today.

As time went on, people started to leave out the minced meat element of mince pies so that by Victorian times, the only ingredient still included that was in any way meat-related was the beef suet that helped to hold the fruit filling together.

Did you know...?

One of the most unusual ingredients put into a mince pie has to be whale meat. James Swan, an American trader, served them up in 1861. They were so popular people demanded seconds!

Despite the best efforts of the Puritans and a change in the shape and ingredients, many superstitions still persist regarding the humble mince pie. One of the most widespread is that you should make a wish as you chow down on your first mince pie of the festive season; indeed, it is unlucky to refuse it when offered! Then there is the belief that mince pies should be eaten in silence – one that's popular with parents of young children, no doubt.

While you are making the mincemeat mixture to fill your homemade mince pies, you should always stir it in a clockwise direction, as to stir it in an anticlockwise direction is to curse yourself with bad luck for the coming year. And then there is the popular practice of eating one mince pie on each of the twelve days of Christmas, with each one being eaten in a different house. If you do this then you will ensure you have good fortune for the next twelve months.

Of course modern tradition has it that mince pies are a particular favourite of that perennial present-giver, Father Christmas. Although, just imagine how he must feel after consuming the estimated 842 million mince pies (one for every home) that are left out for him on Christmas Eve around the world!

H

is for Humble Pie

Anyone who has reason to eat his words by retracting a previous statement, much to his undoubted embarrassment, is said to 'eat humble pie'. But what exactly is humble pie? And why is it considered to be as unpalatable as the bitter taste of enforced repudiation?

In the fourteenth century, the heart, liver and various entrails of animals, especially deer, were referred to as 'numbles'. By the fifteenth century, 'numbles' had become 'umbles', and were used as a standard pie ingredient popular at the Medieval Christmas feast.

Samuel Pepys, in a diary entry dated 5 July 1662, writes about such pies:

> I having some venison given me a day
> or two ago, and so I had a shoulder roasted,
> another baked, and the umbles baked in a pie,
> and all very well done.

The entry for 8 July 1663 also makes reference to this particular menu item:

> Mrs Turner came in and did bring us an
> Umble-pie hot out of her oven, extraordinarily
> good.

The adjective 'humble', meaning 'of lowly rank' or 'having a low estimate of oneself', has nothing to do with deer offal, but is derived from the Latin and Old French words for loins. The similarity of the sound of the words, and the fact that umble pie was often eaten by those of a humble situation in life, is the most likely reason why 'eat humble pie' came to mean being forced to apologise or to admit a fault, which most people would probably find about as palatable as eating an old pie made from Bambi's lower intestines.

Why are carols sung at Christmas time?

Carol-singing as we would recognise it today, dates back to at least the thirteenth century in England, although we might not recognise many of the actual carols from that time. The idea of carolling is now inextricably tied to Christmas, but it should be remembered that carols have been written for many other festivals that occur throughout the year. A song does not even have to have any religious relevance for it to be called a carol.

The word carol comes from the Greek *choros*, meaning 'a dance', via the Latin *choraula* and the French *carole*, which was specifically a ring-dance. The English spelling of 'carol' is first seen in the *Cursor Mundi* dating from around 1300. In this context, a carol was described as 'a ring-dance in which the dancers themselves sing the governing music'.

It is hard to pin down exactly what a carol is – beyond the connection to dancing, although this itself does not really apply to many carols anymore – since the word has been used to refer to such widely varying pieces of music as sacred choral works, connected to the Nativity, to jovial, and distinctly secular, drinking songs. Although most would now agree that a carol is a Christmas song with connections either to the religious side or the pagan aspects of the midwinter festival, at one time such forms of music were condemned by the Church.

The earliest known hymn in honour of the Nativity is '*Jesus refulsit omnium*' (meaning 'Jesus, Light of all the Nations'). It was written by Saint Hilary of Poitiers who died in AD 368. Nativity hymns such as this were solemn affairs and strictly religious. Something more like the carols we know today developed in Italy among the followers of Saint Francis of Assisi.

Having spent much of his youth as a troubadour, Francis decided that the best way to teach people about Jesus Christ was through song. Francis, and the community of friars he founded, set about writing what many consider to be the first true Christmas carols. Some of them were performed around a Nativity scene that Saint Francis set up one Christmas Eve. In 1224, Franciscans brought the carols to England and began to compose new ones in English. The earliest surviving such carol we have written at that time is 'A Child is Boren Amonges Man'.

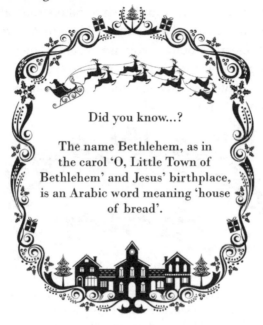

Did you know...?

The name Bethlehem, as in the carol 'O, Little Town of Bethlehem' and Jesus' birthplace, is an Arabic word meaning 'house of bread'.

In thirteenth century England, carols were sung in respectful imitation of the angels who, according to the Gospel writers, sang 'Gloria in excelsis Deo' at Christ's birth. At that time, these religious songs were only sung by the priests and choristers in church.

However, the lyrical content of some carols often incorporated older pagan customs. One such example is the 'Boar's Head Carol'. Others are those about the holly and the ivy, with all their pagan symbolism intact.

The carol also developed hand-in-hand with the mystery play. The 'Coventry Carol' was itself written for one such play, special to the city of Coventry. Some carols were effectively sung narrative poems, such as the 'Cherry Tree Carol', while others interspersed the ballad structure with lines of Latin that all regular church-goers would recognise, even if they didn't actually understand what they meant, as in *'In dulce jubilo'*. (This style is commonplace in many early sixteenth century carols.)

Did you know...?

The 'Cherry Tree Carol' is an example of a carol that tells a story relating to the as yet unborn Christ child. It recounts an apocryphal story of the Virgin Mary. While traveling to Bethlehem, Mary and Joseph stop at a cherry orchard. Mary asks her husband to pick cherries for her, blaming her unborn son for this sudden craving. Joseph rather cruelly tells her to let the child's father pick her cherries. At that moment, Jesus speaks from the womb and commands the cherry tree to lower a branch down to his mother, which it subsequently does. Joseph, in a state of shock, is immediately repentant.

The earliest printed collection of carols was produced by William Caxton's apprentice, and eventual successor, Wynkyn de Worde, in 1521. Richard Kele's *Christmas Carols Newly Imprinted* appeared in 1550, but this particular collection already suffered from the moralising influence of the growing Puritan movement. During the sixteenth and seventeenth centuries, the Puritans made it their mission to take much of the fun out of the festive repertoire. They saw the Christian festival of Christmas as having been corrupted by the more immoral, secular celebrations associated with the season. And they were successful, for a while, too.

As a result, the Puritans did much to put pay to the singing of carols for a good few years. This temporary suppression of the carol was partly as a result of its association with dancing. Where worship out of doors had been perfectly acceptable in the past, the Puritans restrained their worship to the meeting house. Likewise there was no movement allowed within church services; even processions conducted as part of the Sunday service had been removed.

The Puritans also had it in for the mystery plays, for which many of the earlier carols had been written. They did not consider it appropriate to re-enact such holy scenes as Christ's birth, and so in 1642 an 'Order for Stage Plays to Cease' was passed. Songs that suffered as a consequence included the fifteenth century 'Salutation Carol' and the even earlier '*Angelus ad Virginem*', which dated from the middle of the thirteenth century.

Many carols contained the relics of a more

superstitious age, such as *The Holly and the Ivy*, which the Puritans could not tolerate. Only material from the scriptures was considered suitable to be used in songs of worship, so out went such legendary carols as 'The Carnal and the Crane' and 'King Herod and the Cock'.

However, under Puritan rule the carol did not vanish altogether. As long as the songs were holy and sombre affairs, sung with all due reverence, they were acceptable. 1642 saw a collection called *Good and True, Fresh and New Christmas Carols* published, while after the Restoration other collections such as *New Carols for this Merry Time of Christmas* (1661) and *New Christmas Carols* (1662) followed.

By writing their own carols – although they were not what the Medieval merry-makers would have called a carol – the Puritans hoped to convert people to their way of thinking. Nonetheless, many of the carols written at this time are no longer in use today, and with good reason. The majority of them were intended to correct people and improve their lives. Such penitential pieces did not prove very popular. One that has endured, however, is the lullaby 'Wither's Rocking Hymn', written by staunch Puritan George Wither (1588–1667).

Although Christmas carols did not enjoy a massive revival after the Restoration of the monarchy in 1660, at the turn of the eighteenth century new carols were being written. 'While Shepherds Watched' and 'Hark! The Herald Angels Sing' are both from this time. It could be argued that these were not really Christmas carols but Christmas hymns, as was what came after, since the music was no longer suggestive of dancing, whereas 'I Saw Three Ships' (which dates from the Middle Ages) has a galloping rhythm that would have suited a ring-dance very well.

It wasn't until the mid-nineteenth century, though, that the carol, along with the rest of Christmas, enjoyed a more substantial revival, and yet even then, at the beginning, it was mainly thanks to two men in particular. The Reverend John Mason Neale was the Warden of Sackville College, East Grinstead, in Sussex, and a known translator of Greek and Latin hymns. The Reverend Thomas Helmore was Vice-Principal of St Mark's College, Chelsea, and an accomplished musician. These two clergymen worked together on translating and interpreting the sixteenth century tunes found inside what was possibly the only surviving copy of an ancient book called the *Piae Cantiones*, compiled by one Theodoricus Petrus of Nyland, Finland, in 1582.

In 1853, Neale and Helmore published the fruits of their labours in a collection of twelve carols under the title *Carols for Christmas-tide*. The carol 'Unto us a Boy is Born' has been passed on to us from this collection (although it can also be found in a fifteenth century manuscript), as has 'Good King Wenceslas'.

Did you know...?

In this day and age, the Christmas number one is as important to the masses as Christmas carols, and the battle for the festive top slot is a hard fought one. Novelty songs and fund-raising charity songs (which may, or may not, have a Christmas theme) have regularly topped the Christmas charts, with the volume of record sales in the UK peaking at Christmas. This has meant that many of the festive number ones have also garnered the accolade of best-selling song of the year.

The Beatles are the only act to have had four Christmas number ones. This unique accomplishment has helped Sir Paul McCartney to have a Christmas number one on no less than eight occasions, with various different acts, while Sir Cliff Richard has had four; two as a solo act, one with The Shadows and one as part of Band Aid II.

The most unusual Christmas number one has to be that of Rage Against the Machine in 2009. The American rap metal band's single 'Killing in the

Name' (originally released in 1992) outsold Joe McElderry (that year's X Factor winner) as a result of a successful Facebook campaign, which also made RATM the first group to achieve the coveted Christmas number one with a download-only single, and resulted in the most download sales in a single week in UK chart history.

However, the biggest selling UK Christmas number one of all time is the original Band Aid's 'Do They Know It's Christmas?' Written by Bob Geldof and Midge Ure, to raise funds for and awareness of the 1984 Ethiopian famine, this landmark charity single featured an all-star cast (for the time) including members of Culture Club, Spandau Ballet, Duran Duran, Bananarama, U2, The Police, Status Quo, and Genesis. 'Do They Know It's Christmas?' has sold a Santa's sleigh-busting 3.7 million copies to date and is the second biggest selling single of all time (after Elton John's 'Candle in the Wind 1997', released in the wake of the death of Diana, Princess of Wales).

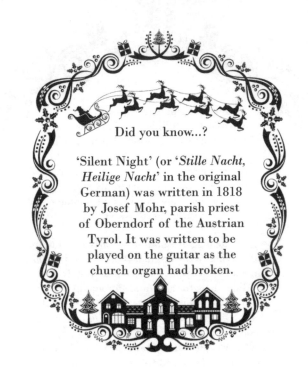

Did you know...?

'Silent Night' (or 'Stille Nacht, Heilige Nacht' in the original German) was written in 1818 by Josef Mohr, parish priest of Oberndorf of the Austrian Tyrol. It was written to be played on the guitar as the church organ had broken.

Seeing the success of Neale and Helmore's work, and the passion with which it was received, others soon followed in their footsteps, bringing out their own carol collections. Many of those sung today were written at the end of the nineteenth century and the beginning of the twentieth. 'See Amid the Winter's Snow', 'Once in Royal David's City', 'In the Bleak Midwinter', and even 'Away in a Manger' were all written at this time.

Some of our most famous carols have their roots in America. During the mid-nineteenth century American composers wrote such carols as 'Away in a Manger' and 'Kings of Orient', which, in turn, influenced the ancient tradition of carol-singing on this side of the Pond.

Carol-singing itself enjoyed a revival during the Victorian era. The long-lasting impact the Puritans had on Christmas meant that carols were not really sung in church again until the 1880s. It was then that the familiar service of nine lessons and carols was drawn up by the Bishop of Truro, E.W. Benson, who later went on to become Archbishop of Canterbury.

New carols are still being written today, of course (along with endless festive pop ditties), but it is the carols of the late-nineteenth century and those that have made it to us from the sixteenth century that are sung every Christmas with the greatest fondness and fervour.

——— The A to Z of Christmas ———

is for Island

As its name might suggest, Christmas Island was discovered on Christmas Day. For centuries, the island's isolation in the middle of the Indian Ocean and its rugged coastline made it a no-go area as far as settlers were concerned. British and Dutch navigators didn't even bother to include the island on their charts until the early seventeenth century. It was one Captain William Mynors, of the East India Ship Company vessel the *Royal Mary*, who named the island when he arrived on Christmas Day, 1643. Even though Captain Mynors named the island, he himself was unable to land there, and it was not until 1688, when the vessel of Captain Charles Swan the reluctant buccaneer, the *Cygnet*, arrived that the first recorded landing took place.

Christmas Island is now a territory of Australia, with a permanent population of just over 2,000, most of whom are Chinese Australian. The summit of a submarine mountain, Christmas Island is dominated by stands of rainforest and more than half of it is protected as an Australian national park Its unusual flora and fauna – including thirteen species of land crabs – are of significant interest to scientists and naturalists.

The coconut crab – also known as the robber crab, or palm thief – is a species of terrestrial hermit crab and is the largest land-living arthropod in the world, growing up to 1 m (3 ft) in length from leg to leg and up to 4.1 kg (9 lb) in weight. Another Christmas Island native is the significantly smaller Christmas Island red crab, with a carapace measuring up to 116 millimetres (4.6 in) in width. The annual mass migration of the red crab sees around 100 million of the crustaceans return to the sea to spawn, and has been called one of the wonders of the natural world.

MERRY CHRISTMAS

When was there a Frost Fair on the River Thames?

It might seem hard to believe now, but between 1400 and 1814 the River Thames froze over completely twenty-six times. And when it froze solid, Londoners made the most of it, holding Frost Fairs on the ice.

The tidal, and even somewhat salty, Thames is a deep, fast-flowing river today. However, before the old London Bridge was demolished in 1831, the river's waters pooled slightly behind its many Medieval arches, which would have helped the ice take hold in the depths of winter. The embankments had not yet been built, either, so the River Thames was wider, shallower, and probably a little slower moving. This period was also the time known as the Little Ice Age, when winters were colder and more severe than they have been since 1800.

The Thames froze several times in Tudor England. Henry VIII is known to have travelled from Whitehall to Greenwich by sleigh, along the River Thames, in 1536. In 1564, Elizabeth I practised her archery on the frozen Thames, whilst menfolk played football on the ice. It was said of this winter:

On the twenty-first of December, began a frost, which continued so extremely that on New Year's Eve people went over and along the Thames on the ice from London Bridge to Westminster. Some played at the foot-ball as boldly there as if it had been on the dry land; diverse of the court shot daily at pricks set up on the Thames; and the people, both men and women, went on the Thames in greater numbers than in any street of the city of London.

On the thirty-first day of January, at night, it began to thaw, and on the fifth day was no ice to be seen between London Bridge and Lambeth, which sudden thaw caused great floods and high waters, that bare down bridges and houses, and drowned many people.

The first frost fair, in terms of full-scale activity and commercial stalls and sports took place in 1608. It was a cheerful and spontaneous affair.

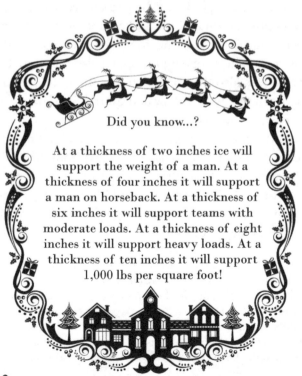

Did you know...?

At a thickness of two inches ice will support the weight of a man. At a thickness of four inches it will support a man on horseback. At a thickness of six inches it will support teams with moderate loads. At a thickness of eight inches it will support heavy loads. At a thickness of ten inches it will support 1,000 lbs per square foot!

The Long Freeze or Great Freeze of 1683/4 was one of the coldest-known European winters. The Thames froze solid, and the ice was up to a foot deep. The frost began six weeks before Christmas, and lasted well into February.

Streets of stalls and booths stretched from bank to bank, with all of London's usual entertainments making their way onto the river. A whole ox was roasted at Hungerford Steps, whilst bear-baiting and puppet-shows were held on the ice. Skating and chair-pushing events were also arranged. A pamphlet published about the Long Frost included this passage:

> A whole street of booths, contiguous to each other, was built from the Temple Stairs to the barge-house in Southwark, which were inhabited by traders of all sorts, which usually frequent fairs and markets, as those who deal in earthenwares, brass, copper, tin, and iron, toys and trifles; and besides these, printers, bakers, cooks, butchers, barbers, coffee-men, and others, who were so frequented by the innumerable concourse of all degrees and qualities, that, by their own confession, they never met elsewhere the same advantages, every one being willing to say they did lay out such and such money on the river of Thames.

The Great Frost of 1709, probably Europe's coldest winter for 500 years, saw another large-scale frost fair. Not only rivers but huge chunks of the North Sea froze, and in France an estimated 500,000 people died of starvation and malnutrition later in the year as a direct consequence. A London paper at the time said:

> The Thames seems now a solid rock of ice; and booths for sale of brandy, wine, ale, and other exhilarating liquors, have been for some time fixed thereon; but now it is in a manner like a town; thousands of people cross it, and with wonder view the mountainous heaps of water that now lie congealed into ice. On Thursday a great cook's-shop was erected, and gentlemen went as frequently to dine there as at any ordinary. Over against Westminster, Whitehall, and Whitefriars, printing presses are kept on the ice.

The last proper freezing of the River Thames in London took place in 1814. The frost set in at the start of January, and by the end of the month, the River was frozen solid. An elephant was even led across the Thames by Blackfriars Bridge to demonstrate the safety of the ice!

Hordes of traders and entertainers rushed to set up shop, and the fair was soon in full-swing. It was shorter than many, as the solid ice lasted only a week. Writing 20 years later, Charles Mackay said of the 1814 fair:

> Each day brought a fresh accession of pedlars to sell their wares, and the greatest rubbish of all sorts was raked up and sold at double and treble the original cost. The watermen profited exceedingly, for each person paid a toll of twopence or threepence before he was admitted to the fair; and something also was expected for permission

to return. Some of them were said to have taken as much as six pounds in a day.

Did you know…?

The largest piece of ice to fall to earth was an ice block 6m (or 20ft) across that fell in Scotland on 13 August 1849. The largest hailstone recorded fell on 14 April 1986 in Bangladesh weighing 1 kg (2.25 lbs). The hailstorm reportedly killed 92 people.

Why are reindeer so associated with Christmas?

It may surprise you to learn that reindeer did not enter the Father Christmas story until the nineteenth century, and it was all the fault of an American Episcopalian minister called Clement Clarke Moore (1779-1863). It was Moore who composed the famous poem 'An Account of a Visit from Saint Nicholas' (a.k.a.

"Twas the Night Before Christmas'), as a Christmas treat for his own children.

In his poem, Moore had a diminutive elf-like Santa pulled in a miniature sleigh by equally tiny reindeer. At one point Santa reels off their now so familiar names, but which were new to those reading the poem when it first appeared in print back in 1823.

More rapid than eagles his coursers they came,
And he whistled, and shouted, and called them by name:
'Now, Dasher! now, Dancer! now, Prancer and Vixen!
On, Comet! on Cupid! on, Donder and Blitzen!'

Moore was embarrassed by his poem, which is wholly secular and mentions nothing of the religious festival that inspired it beyond the name of Saint Nicholas. At first he didn't take credit for it. However, by the 1830s it had really taken off.

With children all over America expectantly awaiting a visit from Santa Claus on Christmas Eve as a result of his poem, Moore eventually decided it was time to come clean. In 1837 he claimed authorship when it was published in a book of poems, and later, in 1844, when it appeared in an anthology of his own work.

What is immediately apparent from a reading of
'An Account of a Visit from Saint Nicholas' is the
complete lack of an appearance by the red-nosed

reindeer himself, Rudolph. That's because he wasn't an invention of Moore but appeared more than 100 years later.

'Rudolph the Red-Nosed Reindeer' first graced the page in 1939. It was a rather whimsical, narrative poem, written with the express intention of drawing more customers into Montgomery Ward stores, and was the creation of Robert L. May, an American copywriter working for the department store chain. The eponymous reindeer subsequently appeared in an advertisement for the Chicago store.

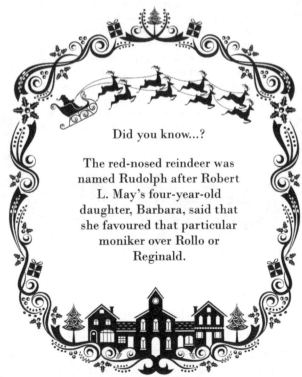

Did you know...?

The red-nosed reindeer was named Rudolph after Robert L. May's four-year-old daughter, Barbara, said that she favoured that particular moniker over Rollo or Reginald.

The child-like character of Rudolph, who ensured that all the good little boys and girls received their presents from Santa one foggy Christmas Eve, struck a chord and survived, in doing so ensuring that Rudolph became as much a part of Christmas as roast turkey and Christmas pudding.

Many people know of 'Rudolph the Red-Nosed Reindeer' in the form of a song, but it wasn't set to music until 1949. The composer was called Johnny Marks and his musical version was recorded by 'the singing cowboy' Gene Autry – a big deal at the time.

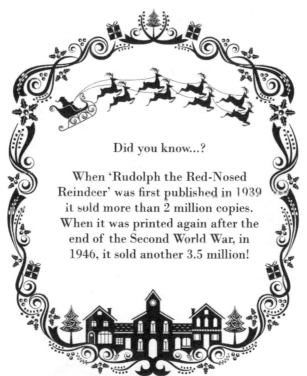

Did you know...?

When 'Rudolph the Red-Nosed Reindeer' was first published in 1939 it sold more than 2 million copies. When it was printed again after the end of the Second World War, in 1946, it sold another 3.5 million!

The song has been recorded by hundreds of other artists since then – including Destiny's Child in 2004, Barry Manilow in 2009, and rapper DMX in 2012 – and has sold more than 80 million records worldwide!

10 things you probably didn't know about Rudolph and his friends

1. The reindeer is the only deer that can be domesticated, and was the first hoofed animal to be domesticated. It provides the nomadic tribes who live within the Arctic Circle (such as the Lapps) with milk, cheese, meat, fat, clothing, footwear, tools (made from the antlers and bones), highly durable bindings (made from the animal's sinews) and a means of transport.

2. The Finns once measured distance in terms of how far a reindeer could run without having to stop to urinate. The *poronkusema* is a measurement somewhere between 7 km and 10 km. The word *poronkusema* itself means 'reindeer peeing'.

3. A reindeer calf can outrun a man at only one day old.

4. Lady reindeer are the only females of any species of deer that have horns.

5. In Iceland, reindeer meat (or *hreindýr*) is becoming an increasingly popular Christmas dinner choice.

6. The Lapp people of Scandinavia believe that taking powdered reindeer antlers increases virility.

7. Reindeer are able to walk over snow without sinking into it because their weight is distributed over a large area thanks to their wide-splayed hooves.

8. One reindeer can pull twice its body weight up to 40 miles.

9. Reindeers are vegetarians by choice but when the supply of greenery runs out they will eat anything, and everything, from eggs and shed antlers, to placenta and even rodents!

10. And lastly, male reindeer lose their antlers in the winter; only the females and castrated males keep them. So either way, it's not looking good for Rudolph! Having a red-nose was the least of his problems...

—— The A to Z of Christmas ——

is for Jingle Bells

A perennial favourite of the Christmas season is the world renowned 'Jingle Bells' – originally called 'One Horse Open Sleigh' – but did you know that the song is actually over 150 years old? It was written by

James Lord Pierpont in 1857 and, at the time, it had a different chorus melody, which was more classical in character. The 1857 lyrics also differed slightly from those we know today.

The song has been translated into many languages and was the first song broadcast from outer space, in a Christmas-themed prank by Gemini 6 astronauts Tom Stafford and Wally Schirra, on 16 December 1965.

On the side of a building in the centre of Medford Square in Medford, Massachusetts, USA, there is a plaque commemorating the birthplace of 'Jingle Bells'. However, in Savannah, Georgia, there is a marker commemorating the composition of 'Jingle Bells' in a church there where Pierpont served as music director.

Who is the real Father Christmas?

Every Christmas Eve, children the world over await the arrival of one individual more than any other (or at least one of his many lieutenants) with excited anticipation. The image of the jolly old man with his long white beard, red suit and attendant reindeer couldn't be more familiar, but where did this admittedly peculiar figure come from? Who is, or was, the real Father Christmas?

Whether you call him Father Christmas, Santa Claus, Sinterklaus or Kris Kringle, the semi-historical, semi-legendary figure who inspired the Christmas gift-giver children know and love today was one Saint Nicholas.

And he didn't come from the North Pole or Lapland. Saint Nicholas came from Turkey (although, of course, turkeys come from Mexico)!

Nicholas was the Greek Orthodox Bishop of Myra in fourth century Byzantine Anatolia. His parents both died when he was still a young man, leaving him a considerable fortune. Shunning his wealth and privileged background to join the Church, Nicholas then made it his mission to give his riches away to those more deserving, and in greater need, than he. The most well-known example of his charity is the one which led to children hanging up their stockings on Christmas Eve for Santa to fill with gifts.

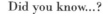

Did you know...?

Santa Claus' official post office is to be found in Rovaniemi, the capital of the Province of Lapland in northern Finland. He receives somewhere in the region of 600,000 letters each year!

Did you know...?

If Santa's sleigh carried just one Barbie doll and one Action Man for every girl and boy on the planet, it would weigh 400,000 tons and need almost 1 billion reindeer to pull it. To deliver all his presents in one global night-time, Santa would have to visit 1,500 homes a second and, allowing for chimney descents and mince pie breaks, he and his reindeer would have to travel at roughly 5,000 times the speed of sound. The sleigh (and its attendant billion reindeer) would behave like a meteorite and burst into flames at a fraction of that speed – about 1/250th of a second – and would burn up in the Earth's atmosphere. Roast reindeer, anyone?

Nicholas is credited with performing various miracles during his lifetime, which have led to him becoming the patron saint of different groups of people. A number of legends tell of how he saved ships and their crews when threatened by storms at sea. As a result he is the patron saint of sailors.

He is also the patron of children. This may be thanks to another story told about him; the miracle of the boys in a barrel. In some versions of the story there are two boys, in others three, but the rest of the details are roughly the same. The story goes that the boys were travelling to Athens, where they were to be educated, but had been told by their father to stop off at Myra on the way to receive the bishop's blessing. When they arrived at the town, night had already fallen and so they took a room at a local inn, intending to visit Nicholas the next morning.

Unfortunately for the boys, the innkeeper decided to rob them, thinking that their possessions would make easy pickings. That night the felon crept into the room where they slept and murdered them where they lay. To hide his heinous crime, and profit still further from the villainous deed, he chopped up their bodies, pickling them in barrels of brine, planning to sell their flesh to his customers as salted pork.

However, Bishop Nicholas learnt that the boys were due to visit him and so set out in search of them. His enquiries eventually brought him to the inn and, when questioned about the boys, the innkeeper panicked, telling Nicholas that the boys had been there but had left the following morning. Nicholas was having none of it and set about searching the premises. It did not take him long to find the barrels which held the boys' dismembered corpses.

With a dramatic change of heart, no doubt brought on by extreme guilt, the innkeeper broke down and confessed his sins, begging the bishop for forgiveness. The saint was utterly convinced by the innkeeper's desire to repent and prayed for both him, and the dead boys. As he concluded his prayer, the body parts reunited and the boys emerged from the brine barrels, alive and wholly intact. And so they continued on their way to Athens.

Did you know...?

It is highly likely that the story of the boys in the barrel came about by mistake. Having given three poor girls the money they needed for their dowries, Nicholas was often represented holding three bags of gold. In some Medieval images these money bags looked more like three balls. The step from balls to heads was not a huge one, but the presence of three heads in iconography of the saint had to be explained somehow, and so the miracle of the boys in the barrel was concocted.

Nicholas is also the protector of the poor, unmarried girls, prostitutes and pawnbrokers, bakers, scholars, Russia, Greece, archers, bankers, Sicily, Naples, jurors, perfumers, brides, robbers, coopers, brewers and travellers. This highly venerated bishop died on 6 December in either AD 326, 345 or 352 – historians aren't certain! As a result, 6 December is his feast day and in some countries it is after sunset on that day that Father Christmas visits children to bestow his gifts.

Did you know...?

During the thirteenth and fourteenth centuries, it was the custom within the great cathedrals to appoint a boy bishop from among the choristers on the feast of Saint Nicholas. Wearing full episcopal garb – mitre and crozier included – his term of office lasted from 6 December until Holy Innocents' Day, 28 December. During this time the boy bishop carried out all the functions of a priest, from taking church services to appointing canons (from among his fellow choristers). This practice began to die out in Tudor times, when both Henry VIII and Elizabeth I tried to ban the potentially blasphemous tradition.

One of the first places to benefit from gifts brought by the saint was the town of Bari in Italy. Pilgrims were big business in the Middle Ages and to attract them a place needed relics, ideally something associated with Christ but, failing that, the earthly remains of a popular saint. In 1097, Norman pirates raided Myra and stole Saint Nicholas' remains from his tomb. The raiders claimed that they were saving the saint from the advancing Muslims but it is more than likely that they were actually motivated by a desire to ensure Bari's future prosperity.

But the image we now have of Father Christmas has its origins in more than just the legendary life of one particular saint. In truth, Father Christmas's origins go back much further than fourth century Turkey. For the Norsemen of Scandinavia, the season of Yule was as much a dark time ruled over by demons and malevolent spirits. It was best to stay indoors, to escape the baleful gaze of the nocturnal flyer Odin. Odin also brought winter to the world. In this guise he was accompanied by his Dark Helper, a demonic horned creature who punished wrong-doers. This figure would resurface later as Father Christmas's assistant.

Thor, the Norse god of thunder, may well have had a hand in influencing the development of the Father Christmas myth, for he rode across the sky in an iron chariot pulled by two huge goats, called Tanngrisnir and Tanngnjóstr (in English, Gnasher and Cracker), rather like Santa's sleigh, with its team of reindeer.

There is also evidence that pagan peoples once worshipped an elemental spirit called Old Man

Winter. He too went into the mix that was to eventually produce the figure of Father Christmas.

Christmas itself has been personified for centuries within the British Isles. In a carol, the words of which were written around the year 1500, he is called 'Sir Christèmas'.

'Nowell, nowell, nowell, nowell.'
'Who is there that singeth so, nowell, nowell, nowell?'
'I am here, Sir Christèmas.'
'Welcome, my lord Sir Christèmas!
Welcome to all, both more and less,
Come near, nowell.'
'Dieu vous garde, beaux sieurs, tidings I you bring:
A maid hath borne a child full young,
Which causeth you to sing, nowell.'
'Christ is now born of a pure maid, born of a pure maid;
In an ox stall he is laid,
Wherefore sing we at a brayed, nowell.'
'Buvez bien, buvez bien par toute la compagnie.
Make good cheer and be right merry,
And sing with us now joyfully, nowell!'

To the Medieval mind there had to be balance in all things. Just as there was Heaven and Hell, rich and poor, Father Christmas couldn't just give to the good and let those who had been bad get off scot free. And so the character of the Dark Helper re-emerged.

Sometimes called Black Peter, under the influence of the Church, the Dark Helper became a demon enslaved by the saint. As well as having horns, he was covered in shaggy black hair, and carried a birch rod with which he would punish naughty children, and also badly behaved women!

Black Peter is known by different names across Europe, but his purpose remains the same: to be the antithesis of Father Christmas. To some he is Pelz Nickel or Klaubauf. To others he is Knecht Reprechte, dressed in animal skins and straw, or even Old Nick, the Devil himself!

People living in the seventeenth century had a different concept of a 'Father Christmas', but he was a figure that oversaw the community celebrations rather than someone who gave presents to children. The modern image we now have of Father Christmas didn't really develop until well into the nineteenth century. Up until that time he had been everything from slim to fat, tall to tiny, elfin, troll-like, a pagan druid, a variation on the spirit of nature in the form of the Green Man (bedecked with garlands of holly, ivy and mistletoe), a drunk (riding in a sleigh pulled by turkeys), and the jolly and generous Lord Christmas.

It was Clement Clarke Moore, the American Episcopalian minister and author of the poem 'An Account of a Visit from Saint Nicholas' (better known by its first line, ''Twas the Night Before Christmas'), who introduced the team of eight reindeer and had Santa gaining entry to the house down the chimney. In fact, American culture has had a huge impact on the development of the modern image of Santa Claus, which originally came to the US from the Netherlands in the guise of Sinterklaus.

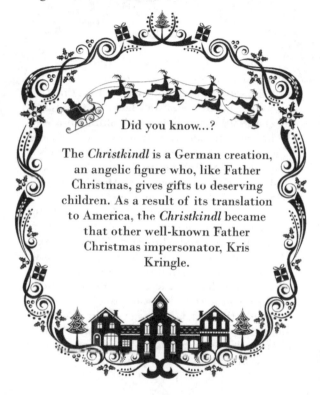

Did you know...?

The *Christkindl* is a German creation, an angelic figure who, like Father Christmas, gives gifts to deserving children. As a result of its translation to America, the *Christkindl* became that other well-known Father Christmas impersonator, Kris Kringle.

The German-American caricaturist Thomas Nast also had his part to play in creating what we would now call the traditional image of Santa Claus. His classic version of the jolly fellow appeared in *Harper's Weekly*, in 1863. Before then, most depictions of Santa had shown him as a tall, thin man. However, Nast drew him as the bearded, plump individual known today.

131

Did you know...?

The Coca-Cola Company's Christmas advertising campaigns have been so successful that some people now believe that Coke actually invented Santa Claus. At the start of the 1930s, Coca-Cola was looking for a way to increase its sales during winter, a slow time for the soft drinks market. The company's answer was to link Santa Claus in the minds of potential customers with their product. Haddon Sundblom, a commercial illustrator, created a series of paintings showing Father Christmas to be a larger-than-life character, wearing a red and white suit. Many believe that Santa wears these colours because they are Coca-Cola's corporate colours. However, the truth is that by the 1920s, the red-suited, white-whiskered, sack-carrying Santa was already the standard image of the seasonal saint. Up until the beginning of the twentieth century, however, Santa could be seen wearing everything from red, to green, to blue – even purple!

So, the Father Christmas – Santa Claus, Kris Kringle, call him what you like – that we know and love today is really an amalgamation of the gift-giving Santa Claus, the personification of the festive season Father Christmas and a fourth century Turkish saint.

Father Christmas is known around the world and, as a consequence, by many different names. In France he is Père Noël, in the Netherlands he is Sinterklaus and in China he is known as Sing Dan Lo Yan (which is literally 'Christmas Old Man').

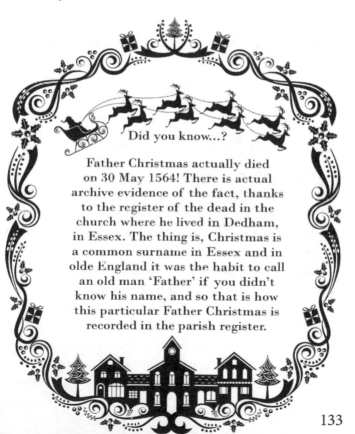

Did you know...?

Father Christmas actually died on 30 May 1564! There is actual archive evidence of the fact, thanks to the register of the dead in the church where he lived in Dedham, in Essex. The thing is, Christmas is a common surname in Essex and in olde England it was the habit to call an old man 'Father' if you didn't know his name, and so that is how this particular Father Christmas is recorded in the parish register.

Although the idea of a beneficent bringer of gifts at Christmas time is almost universal in Christian countries the world over, it isn't always Santa Claus who does the honours. In Spain and South America it is the Three Kings who brings presents, just as they gave gifts to the Christ child. In Russia it is either the grandmotherly Babouschka or Grandfather Frost, while in Scandinavia (for many the home of Santa Claus) gift-giving is the job of a tribe of gnomes, one of whom goes by the name of Julenissen.

—— The A to Z of Christmas ——

is for Krampus

In the twenty-first century, we have become so used to the idea of Santa bringing gifts to good little boys and girls on Christmas Eve it is easy to forget that not so long ago, bad little boys and girls were likewise punished.

In the wild heartlands of Europe such legends are not so easily forgotten, and so it is that in countries such as Austria and Hungary, on 5 December, communities remember Krampus, a demonic anti-Santa who accompanies St. Nicholas during the Christmas season, warning and punishing bad children.

In the Alpine regions, traditionally young men dress

up as the Krampus and roam the streets, frightening children and women with rusty chains and clanging bells. In some rural areas the tradition goes so far as to include the birching of young girls!

Images of Krampus usually show him with a basket on his back, used to carry away bad children and dump them into the pits of Hell. The name Krampus itself originates from the Old High German word *krampen*, meaning 'claw'.

So when the chubby, cheery fellow with the bulging sack of presents asks if you've been good or bad, you had better have been good, for goodness sake…

Why is fish eaten on Christmas Eve?

In many households it is still traditional to eat fish on Christmas Eve; but why?

This custom is one of those that arose during a more religious time in our country's history. During the Middle Ages, it was the tradition to eat fish on a Friday, because Friday was a day of abstinence when the Catholic Church prohibited the consumption of meat, and this is still a not uncommon practice today.

In Catholic countries – and Great Britain was once a Catholic country – the night of 24 December is the Vigil of the Nativity and, as such, is a fast. That being the case, meat is not to be eaten at this time either. However, our Medieval forebears did not consider fish to be meat, and so a fish dish is permissible.

During the reign of King Henry V (he of Agincourt and Sir Lawrence Olivier fame), at one Christmas at court, a huge range of fish was consumed, everything from salmon, lobster and roach, to carp, lampreys and pike!

Special kinds of fish are enjoyed on Christmas Eve throughout Europe. In Brittany, in France, cod is the fish of choice. In many parts of Germany and Styria it is carp, while herring salad is the favoured dish in Saxony and Thuringia. Further afield, in Italy, a great supper – called the *cenone* – has fish at its centre, with stewed eels being particularly popular.

Of course Christmas Eve is probably best known as the night when Father Christmas delivers presents to those children who have been good during the previous year. However, there are many more traditions and customs associated with Christmas Eve above and beyond the visit of poor, over-burdened Santa Claus and his beleaguered team of reindeer.

A custom associated with Christmas Eve peculiar only to England was that of the Dumb Cake. This was a very dumb cake indeed, as it was actually a kind of loaf, baked on Christmas Eve by any single girl who wanted to find out who she was eventually going to marry.

For the magic of the Dumb Cake to work, the desperately seeking singleton had to make the cake alone and in silence. Once done, she pricked it with her initials and then went to bed, but leaving the door open. At the stroke of midnight, her husband-to-be

was supposed to enter the house and prick his ini...
next to hers. A variation on this tradition had t...
young lady's intended entering the house and turnin...
the cake as it cooked in the oven.

Did you know...?

In 1289 the Bishop of Hereford,
Richard de Swinfield, spent Christmas at his
manor of Prestbury, near Gloucester. Christmas Eve
was kept as a fast, as was the tradition, but that didn't
stop the bishop and his household consuming rather a
large amount of food. Herrings, conger eels, codlings
and a salmon were eaten, and 150 large plates, 200
small plates and 300 dishes were required for this
fasting feast.

But that was as nothing compared to what was eaten
from Christmas Day to the feast of Saint John the
Evangelist on 27 December. During those three days,
those spending Christmas at Prestbury managed to put
away one boar, two-and-three-quarter cows, two calves,
four doves, four pigs, 60 chickens and capons, eight
partridges and two geese, and still found room for bread
and cheese. Forty gallons of red wine were quaffed,
along with four gallons of white wine. How much ale
(which was everyone's everyday beverage) was drunk
is not recorded!

...ristmas Eve has also long been the traditional ...e to decorate the house and put up the tree ready ...r Christmas morning. However, in our modern age it is a well-documented fact that Christmas starts earlier and earlier each year, so that trees and decorations festoon streets and department stores from as early as the beginning of October.

For many people Christmas celebrations themselves start on Christmas Eve. For some nationalities, such as the people of Poland, it is the time when families gather to exchange gifts. For others, Christmas starts with Midnight Mass on Christmas Eve. At this time, bells are sometimes tolled to announce the death of the Devil and the coming of Christ.

Did you know...?

The Devil's Knell of Dewsbury in Yorkshire is a very special tolling. Each Christmas Eve the tenor bell of All Saints Parish Church, known as 'Black Tom', is tolled once for every year since Christ's birth in the minutes leading up to Christmas. At midnight all the bells ring out in joyful celebration of the Devil's death!

Did you know...?

In 1867, Macy's department store in New York City remained open until midnight on Christmas Eve for the first time, effectively initiating the tradition of last-minute Christmas shopping.

Midnight is usually known as the witching hour, when fell powers are believed to hold sway over the land, but this rule is turned on its head on Christmas Eve. Evil spirits lose their powers and one Irish legend has it that at that time the gates of Heaven open so that anyone who dies at that selfsame hour will go straight to heaven, rather than having to wait until the last trump of Doomsday.

is for La Befana

In Italy Father Christmas has sub-contracted his gift-giving duties to a kindly old witch called La Befana, who gives children sweets if they've been good and a piece of coal if they haven't.

According to the Italian legend of La Befana, the three wise men stopped at her home on their way to pay homage to the Christ child, and invited her to go with them. But La Befana had lost her own child to the plague and found the prospect of seeing another baby too upsetting.

But after the wise men had left she changed her mind. She set of in pursuit on her broomstick (as you do when you're a witch) but never found the Magi again. Instead, every time she came across a good child's stocking she filled it with toys and sweets in an effort to make amends for her foolishness.

Where does the Christmas crib come from?

Nowadays, the sight of a Nativity scene with the baby Jesus, Mary, Joseph and assorted livestock, alongside visiting herdsmen and foreign dignitaries, is indelibly etched on to the memory of anyone who has grown up in the United Kingdom. Many homes dust off the figures of their own crib scene when they bring out the rest of their Christmas decorations. It can be seen in shopping centres and on the streets of towns up and down the country – not to mention on endless Christmas cards – and is an expected element of any church. There are even specific crib services held on or around Christmas Eve.

In one sense it is very obvious how such a tradition arose, when you consider the 'facts' of the Christmas story told and re-told year after year. But in another way, it might seem a curious practice to keep up when so few people actually attend church on Christmas Day, as its religious significance continues to diminish in the modern age.

The first Nativity scene, created inside a church, was in Rome in the tenth century, at the Church of Santa Maria Maggiore. The idea soon caught on and other churches began creating their own stable scenes in time for the feast of Christ's Mass.

However, one man is credited with creating the

Christmas crib more than any other, and that is the thirteenth century Saint Francis of Assisi. In 1220, Francis made the pilgrimage to Bethlehem. While there, he saw how Christmas was celebrated in the town of Jesus' birth and was so impressed that he asked the Pope, Honorious III, if he might recreate something like it in his own Italian home of Greccio.

With the help of a local landowner, Giovanni Velita, and his friends, Francis succeeded in creating his own representation of the Nativity in a cave, surrounded by candles. Details over the actual participants in his Nativity scene vary, with some saying that Francis used statues to represent the holy family, while others claim that real people, dressed in appropriate costumes, fulfilled the role. However, all the sources agree on the fact that at the centre of the scene was a straw-filled manger surrounded by real animals.

The people of Greccio came to the cave at nightfall on Christmas Eve, bearing candles and torches before them, to attend a Mass held there by Saint Francis. Saint Bonaventure, Francis' biographer, recounts how the experience was incredibly moving for those present to the point where the people were, 'filled with the utmost joy, and shedding tears of devotion and compassion'.

After Saint Francis' death, the custom of having a Christmas crib spread throughout Europe, with smaller wooden Nativity scenes popping up in churches and homes across the continent. By the seventeenth century, the custom of having a representation of the crib in the home was well-established and highly popular. In

England it was even enhanced by the baking of cr-
pies – precursors of the modern mince pie – made in
the shape of a cradle and sometimes with the addition
of a little pastry baby Jesus.

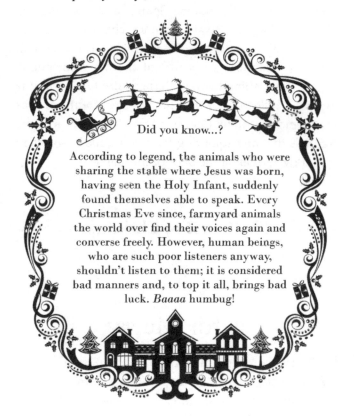

Did you know...?

According to legend, the animals who were
sharing the stable where Jesus was born,
having seen the Holy Infant, suddenly
found themselves able to speak. Every
Christmas Eve since, farmyard animals
the world over find their voices again and
converse freely. However, human beings,
who are such poor listeners anyway,
shouldn't listen to them; it is considered
bad manners and, to top it all, brings bad
luck. *Baaaa* humbug!

Crib scenes almost always have the holy family of
Mary, Joseph and the infant Jesus in either a barn or
a cave, with a donkey and ox present. On top of that
there may also be a couple of shepherds in attendance,

ong with a lamb, and the three wise men. Some scenes even go to the lengths of adding a camel for the travellers from distant lands, a smattering of angels and possibly the Star of Bethlehem shining overhead.

However, in Catalonia, Spain, and the Basque Country, there is always another character present, without fail; the *caganer*. This grotesque individual, who is sometimes a caricature of an unpopular public figure, has nothing to do with the Nativity story but is merely a reflection of the Catalan irreverent sense of scatological humour. *Caganer* means 'crapper', and the figure is that of a squatting man doing his business in the straw, hidden at the back of the stable.

––––––– The A to Z of Christmas –––––––

is for Merry

The word 'merry' now has all sorts of connotations connected with it to do with being slightly intoxicated, but how did the seasonal salutation come to be in the first place? And for how long have Christmases been merry?

'A Merry Christmas and a Happy New Year to You'

was the verse that Sir Henry Cole chose to put on his first commercially available Christmas card in 1843, although the phrase was already in use almost 300 hundred years before that, appearing as it does in *The Hereford Municipal Manuscript* of 1565:

> And thus I comytt you to god, who send
> you a mery Christmas & many.

The word 'merry' has its origins in the Old English word *myrige*, meaning 'pleasing' or 'delightful'. By the sixteenth century there were a number of phrases in everyday use that included the word – 'make merry' (circa 1300), 'Merry England' (circa 1400) and 'the merry month of May' (1560s) – in which it meant 'pleasant' or 'agreeable'. However, by the nineteenth century it had taken on its more familiar meaning of 'jovial and outgoing'.

Another familiar Christmas usage of the word 'merry' is in the English carol 'God Rest Ye Merry, Gentlemen', first published in William Sandys' *Christmas Carols Ancient and Modern* in 1833. The carol probably existed as a folk-song long before it was written down, and the phrase 'rest you merry' appears in *The Dictionary of syr Thomas Eliot knyght* , of 1538:

> Aye, bee thou gladde: or joyfull, as the
> vulgare people saie Reste you mery.

In the context of the carol, 'to rest' means 'to keep, or remain as you are' (rather than 'to repose'), as in the phrase 'rest assured'.

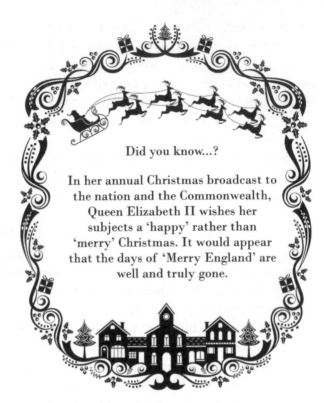

What was the First Noël?

The first Nowell the angel did say
Was to certain poor shepherds in fields as they lay;
In fields where they lay tending their sheep,
On a cold winter's night that was so deep.

Nowell, Nowell, Nowell, Nowell,

Born is the King of Israel.

We hear it sung of in carols every year, from the

familiar 'The First Nowell' to the obscure, such as 'Sir Christèmas', but what does Noël mean? And what was the first one?

Delving into the origins of 'The First Nowell' raises almost as many questions as it answers. Certainly there is much uncertainty as to the carol's origins, as well as the uncertainty regarding the meaning and origin of the word 'Nowell'.

Some believe that the English word 'Nowell' comes from the French *Noël* meaning 'Christmas', which is itself from the Latin *natalis*, meaning 'birth'. However, others believe that *Noël* is actually the French version of the English 'Nowell', which they believe comes from the Anglo-Saxon, and means 'now all is well.'

Then again, it may also originate from two Gaulish words, *noio* or *neu* (both meaning 'new') and *helle* (meaning 'light') and instead refers to the winter solstice, after which the days start to lengthen again, with sunlight banishing the darkness. Or perhaps it is a combination of all of these.

So, in the context of the carol, it would appear that the angel was telling the shepherds that all was now well because the Christ child had been born. But whatever its meaning, 'The First Nowell' surely refers to the first ever Christmas, when Jesus Christ was born (even though he probably wasn't born in the middle of winter at all), and the first Nowell itself, was the first time that God announced to the faithful through his divine messenger that all was well. Take your pick.

It is harder to pinpoint the origins of the carol, however. It is generally considered to have been written in or around the sixteenth or seventeenth century, although it could date from as far back as the thirteenth century, and its actual author remains unknown. The song was at first handed down orally and didn't appear in print until the 1800s. The familiar form of the carol that everyone knows today actually originated in Cornwall, appearing in *Some Ancient Christmas Carols* ten years before *Gilbert and Sandys Christmas Carols* (1833). This later collection was edited by William B. Sandys, while the carols were arranged and edited by Davies Gilbert, who also wrote extra lyrics for some of them. The melody is believed to be a corruption of an earlier tune that would have been sung in a church gallery during services.

The composer Ralph Vaughan Williams notably included 'The First Nowell' in the concluding movement of his 'Christmas masque' *On Christmas Night* (which was based upon Dickens' *A Christmas Carol*) and his Nativity play *The First Nowell.*

Of course, the true stars of the carol are the shepherds to whom the angel makes its special announcement in the first verse. These shepherds represent the common man and particularly the Gentiles (those people who are not Jewish), which is why they play such an important role in the Christmas story.

However, in the first printed version of the carol, the line actually states that there were 'three poor shepherds'. Legends surround the identity of these individuals, just as there are stories told regarding the identity of the three wise men.

In his own note on the text of the carol, William

Sandys' remarks:

> According to some legends, the number [of shepherds] was four, called Misael, Achael, Cyriacus, and Stephanus, and these, with the names of the three Kings, were used as a charm to cure the biting of serpents, and other venomous reptiles and beasts.

Something to bear in mind next time you take a stroll through adder country.

What have holly and ivy got to do with Christmas?

Well, of course for starters there's the popular carol 'The Holly and the Ivy' that's sung at Christmas.

> *The holly and the ivy*
>
> *When they are both full grown;*
>
> *Of all the trees that are in the wood*
>
> *The holly bears the crown.*
>
> *O the rising of the sun*
>
> *And the running of the dear,*
>
> *The playing of the merry organ,*
>
> *Sweet singing in the choir.*
>
> *The holly bears a blossom*
>
> *As white as any flower;*
>
> *And Mary bore sweet Jesus Christ*

To be our sweet saviour.

The holly bears a berry

As red as any blood;

And Mary bore sweet Jesus Christ

To do poor sinners good.

The holly bears a prickle

As sharp as any thorn;

And Mary bore sweet Jesus Christ

On Christmas Day in the morn.

The holly bears a bark

As bitt'r as any gall;

And Mary bore sweet Jesus Christ

For to redeem us all.

Although this oh-so familiar carol is called 'The Holly and the Ivy' when you come to look at it, it is blatantly only about the holly. But that still doesn't explain why both holly and ivy have become so inextricably connected with Christmas.

The main reason is that they are both evergreens, like the fir tree and the boughs used to form the traditional Christmas wreath and, as such, date back to pagan times. The Romans believed both holly and ivy brought good luck and so decorated their homes with the plants during the festival of Saturnalia. They would also give sprigs of the plants to friends and loved ones as good luck tokens.

In time, the Church took these traditional elements of the extant winter festivals and gave them a Christian twist, adding their own symbolism. The sharp leaves of the holly came to represent Christ's crown of thorns, while the red berries were drops of his blood. The nascent Church was so successful in modifying the symbolism of the holly that in Scandinavia it is still known as the 'Christ-thorn'.

Other legends were invented, linking Christ to the holly. One stated that there had been a holly tree growing outside the stable where the infant Jesus was born. The tree was bare of berries, hungry birds having eaten them all. However, as soon as Jesus was born the tree grew new buds again, then flowers and finally berries – all in the space of that one night.

Another tale had it that the shepherds who visited the infant Christ left behind a lamb as a gift, corralling it within a pen of holly branches. The lamb had other ideas, however, and forced its way out of the enclosure to return to the hill pastures with its mother. In doing so, the poor thing tore its coat, the sharp prickles of the holly drawing blood from the creature. It being a cold night, the drops of blood froze becoming the holly's red berries.

To the Medieval mind, the holly and the ivy had other important characteristics. The holly represented the male – with its tough, woody stems and sharp prickles – whilst the ivy was supposed to be female – clinging and feeble. People believed that whichever plant was brought into the house first on Christmas Eve (as it was unlucky to bring either into your home *before* then) would be in charge for the following year. If the holly was brought in first, the man would be the boss, but if the ivy entered before the holly, the woman would be head of the household.

Holly was the more important of the two plants. It was supposed to protect a home from lightning, and so was often planted outside the front door. And it had even more miraculous powers; its red berries were able to detect evil and so the holly could offer protection against witches. Medieval men also believed it had powers like those purported to be possessed by certain deodorant sprays today; carrying the leaves or berries about his person supposedly made a young man irresistible to the ladies.

And of course, in the carol 'The Holly and the Ivy', the point is made none-too-subtly that the plant that represents the male is the most important! However, there were a number of carols written in the fifteenth century that had a different emphasis, although the ivy still often came off the worst.

—— The A to Z of Christmas ——

is for Nutcracker

At Christmas time it is not uncommon for many families to attend the only ballet they will see all year. The name of that ballet? *The Nutcracker*. But how did a ballet about a mechanical device for cracking nuts become such a popular festive tradition?

The story itself upon which the ballet it based – 'The Nutcracker and the King of Mice' by E. T. A. Hoffman – is older than the version we see portrayed on stage, which is actually an adaptation by the French author Alexandre Dumas, better known for penning such classic novels as *The Three Musketeers* and *The Count of Monte Cristo*.

The Nutcracker was actually Peter Ilyich Tchaikovsky's final and least satisfying ballet, after he took on the project with a marked lack of enthusiasm. It is ironic then that it is *The Nutcracker* that has become one of the most beloved Christmas traditions of the modern age.

The Nutcracker premiered in Tchaikovsky's native Russia in 1892, but it wasn't until 1944 that an American ballet company decided to perform the entire thing. That year, the San Francisco Ballet took on the task, from then on performing *The Nutcracker* as an annual tradition.

But it was really George Balanchine who set *The Nutcracker* on the path to popular fame. In 1954 he choreographed the ballet for a New York company, and not a year has passed since when the ballet has not been performed in New York City.

What does a boar's head have to do with Christmas?

The parading in of the boar's head is a tradition dating from at least the fourteenth century, and is still practised in some rarefied institutions today. What's more, it is the origin of the traditional Christmas ham!

However, the presence of a boar's head at the Christmas feast table pre-dates even the establishment of that particular tradition. It was probably begun by the Anglo-Saxons, but the written records mentioning it come mainly from the Middle Ages.

Certainly, in Norse tradition, the sacrifice of an animal was intended to implore Freyr, god of agriculture and fertility (after whom Friday is named), to give his blessing to the year ahead. Swine were chosen for the sacrifice as they were sacred to Freyr. The boar's head itself became a symbol of this sacrifice and the hoped-for harvest.

Of course, it also made a lot of agricultural sense to slaughter most domesticated animals at the start of winter; otherwise they would have to be fed throughout the lean winter months. What with all the fresh meat on offer, and with the harvests having been brought in during the autumn, the end of the year was the ideal time to have a feast.

In both Scandinavia and England, Saint Stephen (he of Good King Wenceslas fame whose feast day falls on Boxing Day) seemed to inherit Freyr's legacy. In old Swedish art Stephen is shown bringing a boar's head to a Yuletide feast. The Christmas ham is not unique to the British Isles either; in Sweden it is an old tradition again linked to the winter solstice boar sacrifice.

During the Middle Ages, a popular Christmas sport was boar-hunting and there was good reason for this.

Wild boars are ferocious animals and in Medieval England they were a genuine menace to humans. Boar was widely hunted and so became the staple of Medieval banquets. It was even considered more of a delicacy than suckling pig. In fact, the animal was so widely hunted that by the sixteenth century it had become extinct in England.

In time, the serving of the boar's head at the Christmas feast came to symbolise Christ's triumph over sin. The boar's head was then carried into the banqueting hall, heralded by great trumpet fanfares and borne aloft upon a gold or silver platter with an apple in its mouth, while minstrels sang in celebration of it. It was decorated with rosemary and bay, and would have formed the centrepiece of the Christmas feast up until the time of Elizabeth I.

Geoffrey Chaucer, the famous fourteenth century English poet, made a passing reference to the boar's head in *The Canterbury Tales*.

> Janus sits by the fire with double beard,
> And drinketh of his bugle horn the wine:
> Before him stands the brawn of tusked swine,
> And 'Nowel' cryeth every lusty man.

Unsurprisingly, the 'Boar's Head Carol' dates from this period as well. It describes the ancient tradition of sacrificing a boar and having its head presented at a Yuletide feast. The surviving version that is most well-known today comes from *Wynkyn de Worde's Christmasse Carolles*, published in 1521.

> *The boar's head in hand I bring*

With garlands gay and birds singing.
I pray you all, help me to sing
Qui estis in convivio!

The boar's head I understand
Is chief service in this land.
Wheresoever it is found,
Seruitur cum sinapio!

The boar's head I dare well say
Anon after the twelfth day,
He takes his leave and goes away,
Exiuit tunc de patria!

The Latin lines translate as follows: *Qui estis in convivio* means 'all who are at this banquet'; *Seruitur cum sinapio* is 'it is served with mustard'; while *Exiuit tunc de patria* means, 'He went out from his native country'.

Probably the best known surviving practice of the tradition is that of the Boars' Head Feast, still held at The Queen's College, Oxford, having started in 1341. This annual event is supposed to commemorate the valorous act once performed by a student of the college.

The young man was walking in Shotover forest, with his head in a book of Aristotle's works, when he was suddenly attacked by a wild boar. The furious beast came at him with its mouth wide open, ready to savage him with its tusks. In an example of astonishingly quick thinking, the youth bravely rammed the book down the boar's throat with a cry of *'Graecum est!'*, which means 'It is Greek!'. The boar promptly choked to death.

At Queen's College this variation of the 'Boar's Head Carol' is sung as the head it brought in:

> *The boar's head in hand bring I*
> *Bedeck'd with bays and rosemary.*
> *I pray you, my masters, be merry*
> *Quot estis in convivio.*
>
> *Caput apri defero*
> *Reddens laudes Domino.*
>
> *The boar's head, as I understand*
> *Is the rarest dish in all this land*
> *Which thus bedeck'd with a gay garland*
> *Let us servire cantico.*
>
> *Caput apri defero*
> *Reddens laudes Domino.*
>
> *Our steward hath provided this*
> *In honour of the King of Bliss;*
> *Which, on this day to be served is*
> *In Reginensi atrio.*
>
> *Caput apri defero*
> *Reddens laudes Domino.*

In this version the Latin translates thus: *Quot estis in convivio* is 'all who are feasting together'; *servite cantico* means 'serve it while singing'; *In Reginensi*

Atrio is 'within the Queen's Hall'; and *Caput apri defero, Reddens laudes Domino* translates as 'I bring the boar's head, sing thanks to the Lord'.

However, although it might be the most famous, it is not only Queen's College, Oxford, that maintains the tradition. Hurstpierpoint College, West Sussex, also holds an annual Boar's Head feast, which has been observed almost since the College's foundation in 1849. The feast celebrates the work done by the College's Sacristans and Choir, with the boar's head being immediately followed by a pot of mustard as it is carried to the dining hall. Then there is the Stourbridge Old Edwardian Club, whose Boar's Head supper has been held every Christmas Eve since 1911. Brawn-filled bread rolls are always on the menu at this particular meal.

The Vicomte de Mauduit wrote about the boar's head, including his own authentic recipe for it. If you would like to serve boar's head this Christmas instead of the usual boiled ham, this is what you should do (according to the Vicomte).

> Bone the head, leaving only the jawbones (for shape) and tusks. Make a small quantity of stuffing composed of minced pig's liver, chopped apples, a little onion, sage and rosemary. Arrange this stuffing all around the inside of the head about half an inch in thickness. Now stuff the rest of the inside of the head with a second stuffing made of sausage meat, squares of ox tongue, chopped truffles, chopped apples, chopped mushrooms, chopped pistachio nuts and minced rosemary.

Add one wineglass of Calvados (or sherry)
and an equal quantity of cream.

When the head is filled tight with this, stitch a ve.
strong cloth over the stuffing, then bind the whole
head in another strong cloth, and put it in a large pot
of boiling water to boil slowly for about eight to nine
hours, during which time you add more boiling water
as evaporation requires. When the head is cooked and
is still warm reshape in cloth, remove the wrapping
and let it get cold.

The ears, which have been cut off and boiled
separately, are then replaced on the head with a
skewer. Place the head on an oblong dish, surround it
with slices of truffles, slices of apples, and strew with
rosemary.

—— The A to Z of Christmas ——

is for Overindulgence

Surveys have shown that on average we will each
eat our way through as many as 6,000 calories on
Christmas Day alone which, according to the British
Dietetic Association, may be a result of overindulging
on second helpings, snacks and alcohol.

Whilst we are likely to put on an average 5 lbs (2 kg)
in weight over the Christmas period, the Christmas

...tself is not the main culprit. In fact, the traditional ...ey roast can be very good for you. The problem is ...at over Christmas we can eat roughly three to four ...imes more food than we actually need. Consequently we end up seeing the New Year in weighing a lot more than we did at the beginning of December. It also means we are storing up problems for the future. After all, the extra calories have to go somewhere and will be laid down as fat, and it's those extra few pounds that can do you harm in the long term.

So what does the average Christmas Dinner mean for our bodies? Here are the nutritional facts. A traditional meal of roast turkey, stuffing, bread sauce, roast potatoes, roast parsnips, boiled carrots, Brussel sprouts, gravy, cranberry sauce, pork sausage, and bacon, provides the diner with 956 calories and 48 g of fat. However, add to that the equally traditional treats of a slice of Christmas cake, another of chocolate log, one serving of cheese and biscuits, a handful of mixed nuts, one portion of Christmas pudding (with custard and brandy butter), just the one mince pie (with double cream), and one glass of mulled wine, and you've added another 2,187 calories and 107 g of fat to your consumption for the day, bringing your total intake to a belt-busting 3,143 calories and an artery-hardening 155 g of fat. And that doesn't include the chocolate orange that Santa left you in your stocking!

Of course there are plenty of ways of ensuring that you don't overindulge over Christmas, but what would be the fun in that?

What is a Christingle?

The making of Christingles and the Christingle service have become a regular fixture in the days leading up to Christmas, usually undertaken by Primary school children. But what actually is a Christingle?

The physical form of a Christingle is an orange, tied with a red ribbon and stuck with a candle, and cocktail sticks bearing fruit and nuts. It is a symbolic object particularly used in Christian Advent services, hence the name given to a particular type of religious service.

First there is the orange; this represents the world. The red ribbon tied around its middle is the blood of Jesus Christ, shed for the sins of mankind. The fruits – usually raisins and cherries – and nuts skewered onto four cocktail sticks represent the fruits of the earth and the four seasons. And lastly, the lighted candle at its centre is a representation of Christ.

The word Christingle actually means 'Christ Light'. Both the Christingles that are made and the Christingle services that take place in church, celebrate Jesus coming into the world, in his aspect as the Light of the World. At Christingle services, the focus is traditionally on children, and such services are seen by many as an opportunity to bring friends and family members of all ages together in worship.

The first Christingle service was held in a castle in Germany, on Christmas Eve 1747, by a bishop of the Moravian Church. The bishop, one Pastor John, wanted to find some simple way of teaching people about the true meaning of Christmas and of the love of Jesus. His solution was to prepare a simple symbol which would make the Christmas message seem fresh and alive to them. During the informal service, Pastor John gave each child present a lighted candle wrapped in a red ribbon. He then intoned a prayer, saying 'Lord Jesus, kindle a flame in these dear children's hearts'.

This custom of distributing lighted candles to children on Christmas Eve, as a reminder that Christ came into the world to be the Light of the World, continued for many years. However, the idea of the Christingle wasn't introduced into the Church of England until 1968. This time it was the brainchild of John Pensom, of The Children's Society, with Pastor John's original ribbon-tied candle having evolved into the decorated orange we know today.

The precise symbolism of the Christingle varies according to when the Christingle service is held. If it is held during Advent, in the lead up to Christmas, it represents the hope of light in the darkness. If the service happens much closer to Christmas Day, such as on Christmas Eve, the Christingle symbolises the birth of Jesus. And if the ceremony doesn't happen until Epiphany, then it stands as an image of the gift of God's light for all the peoples of the world.

What is mulled wine?

There's nothing quite like a little of your favourite tipple to warm your cockles, and when you've been out in the cold of a December night carol-singing nothing warms the cockles quite like a glass of mulled wine.

Mulled wine has a long history, being lauded in Europe since at least the fifth century AD, and appearing in various forms in cook books from the sixteenth century onwards. To 'mull' means 'to heat and spice', although the origin of the word is uncertain. There is a Middle English word, *mollen*, which means 'to moisten' or 'crumble', but how this might connect with heating and spicing things up isn't clear.

It's not just wine that can be mulled of course. Other traditional mulling recipes include those for mead, cider and beer. Mulled wine and mulled beer used to be heated by plunging a red hot poker from the fire into the liquid in question!

It is worth remembering that the 'mull' should never be allowed to get too hot and should most definitely never boil, otherwise the flavour will be spoiled and, worse than that, the alcohol will evaporate.

In Medieval times, people enjoyed a mulled drink called Ypocras, Hipocris or Hippocras. It was named after the Greek physician Hippocrates, dubbed the 'Father of Medicine', who was supposed to have devised the first recipe for it.

During the Middle Ages, Hippocrates had an almost mythical reputation for being able to heal – more magic and mysticism than medicine. As a consequence, Ypocras itself was generally accepted as being some kind of magical elixir for maintaining good health in general, with doctors recommending that it be enjoyed at the end of a meal as an aid to digestion.

Ypocras, and other drinks like it, were believed to be particularly good for keeping away all manner of ills throughout the cold winter months. There is probably some truth in this, for at the time it was certainly safer to drink the wine than the water. The practice of heating the drink would have helped to kill off many of the unpleasant microbes merrily creating their own bit of culture within the wine. And wine did have a tendency to go bad: adding spices and honey would have made it palatable again.

The following is a modern take on the recipe for making this popular Medieval drink:

Ypocras

1 bottle of sweet red or white wine

1–2 cups of honey

1 tbs each of ginger, cinnamon, cardamom, white pepper, cloves, nutmeg, and caraway seeds

A cheesecloth

Bring the wine and honey close to the boil in a pan, skimming off the scum as it rises to the surface. Taste the concoction and add more honey to sweeten, if desired. Take off the heat and stir in the spices. Leave it to sit for 24 hours, while covered. During this time the spices form a thick residue at the bottom of the pan. Now, using a ladle, decant the wine into a second container, straining it through 2–3 layers of cheesecloth, while trying to leave as much of the spice residue in the pan as possible. Store for 1 month before serving – the older it is, the better it tastes!

By the 1500s, recipes began to appear in cookbooks for mulling Clarrey (also spelt 'clarree' or 'claree'), another drink made using wine, honey and spices. Both Clarrey and Ypocras are mentioned by the fourteenth century poet Geoffrey Chaucer. From *The Merchant's Tale* we get the following rhyming couplet:

He drynketh ypocras, clarree, and vernage

Of spices hot, to increase his courage.

The name comes from the Latin *vinum claratum*, meaning 'clarified wine' and it lives on today as 'claret', which is a dry red wine. The original Clarrey, however, can be made with either red or white wine, as it is in this particular recipe.

Clarrey

1 bottle of inexpensive, sweet white wine

1–2 cups of honey

1 tbs each of cinnamon, galingale (or you could substitute ginger) and cardamom

1 tsp of white pepper

A cheesecloth

Bring the wine and honey close to the boil, then reduce the heat and skim off the scum as it rises. Taste and add honey for sweetness as required. Remove from the heat, stir in all of the spices, and then cover and allow to sit for 24 hours. As with the Ypocras, after this time you will need to use a ladle to transfer the liquid into another container, passing it through a strainer lined with 2–3 layers of cheesecloth to remove the spices. Again, leave as much of the spice residue that will have formed in the bottom of the pot behind as possible. Bottle it and store for 1 month before serving. A good Clarrey is one that has been aged for a year or even longer.

Bishop's punch – once called 'bischopswyn' – is a traditional Christmas drink associated with Ol' Saint Nick. In countries where the feast day of Saint Nicholas is observed on 6 December, such as in the Netherlands, revellers use it to toast the original Father Christmas. If you fancy doing the same, try this recipe.

Bishop's Wine

1 bottle of red wine

1 orange stuck with cloves

1 cinnamon stick

The peel of 1 lemon

Sugar to taste

Place the clove-stuck orange in a large pan;

add the red wine and leave to steep for half a day. During this time the wine will take on the flavours of the orange and cloves. Then you need to add the other ingredients together and simply warm the whole lot through half an hour before serving.

Popular in Sweden, Norway, Denmark, Finland and Estonia, and drunk during Advent, *Glögg* is the Scandinavian form of mulled wine. Made from red wine, spices and sugar, it can also have stronger spirits such as brandy, akvavit or vodka added to it. It is served with raisins, almonds and gingerbread biscuits.

Glögg can be made as a non-alcoholic drink, either by boiling it to evaporate the alcohol or by replacing the wine with blackcurrant juice. However, in the recipe presented here, the alcohol remains very much intact.

Glögg

1 bottle of red wine
25 g/1 oz dried orange zest
25 g/1 oz cinnamon sticks
20 cardamom seeds
12 cloves
200 g/8 oz blanched almonds
200 g/8 oz raisins
225 g/½ lb brown sugar

70 ml/2½ fl oz brandy

A cheesecloth

Bring the wine close to the boil in a pot. Put the orange, cinnamon, cardamom and cloves in the cheesecloth, tie it into a bundle and stew it in a pot for 15 minutes. Add the almonds and raisins, and cook for another 15 minutes, before removing the pan from the heat. Add the brown sugar and brandy, and stir them in. Then remove the spice bundle. Serve hot.

Of course the ultimate non-alcoholic winter warmer surely has to be a mug of luxurious hot chocolate. If you're a chocoholic, or at least possessed of a sweet tooth, then you might want to try this particular recipe this Christmas.

Hot Chocolate

570 ml/1 pint milk (whole or semi-skimmed)

140ml/5 fl oz double cream

100 g/4 oz chopped plain chocolate

sugar

Heat the milk and cream in a saucepan until boiling. Take it off the heat and add the chopped chocolate pieces, stirring until all the chocolate has melted. Whisk the hot chocolate until it is smooth, adding sugar to taste, and then pour into warmed mugs to serve.

Why not try flavouring your hot chocolate with a cinnamon stick, vanilla (pods or essence), or a few drops of orange essence? A dusting of cocoa powder or freshly grated nutmeg will finish it off nicely, as will a handful of gooey marshmallows.

———— The A to Z of Christmas ————

P.

is for Presents

Every year, in imitation of the three wise men and Santa Claus, people give gifts to their loved ones at Christmas time. Although gift-giving might involve an expectation of reciprocity (a situation once bemoaned of by Dr Sheldon Cooper in an episode of hit US geek comedy The Big Bang Theory), a present is meant to be free. However, when it comes to gift-giving people effectively agree to honour the terms of a long-established social contract and not to give anything in return is most definitely frowned upon. (It might be better to give than to receive, but just try telling your children on Christmas Day that Santa's stocking is enough for this year.)

Of course, the joy of opening presents on Christmas Day is tinged by the fear that you might receive something you really don't want, such as a pair of Rudolph the Red-Nosed Reindeer slippers, a jumper knitted by granny three sizes too big, or Susan Boyle's 2010 album 'The Gift', which was the first Christmas album ever to top the charts in the UK. (There must have been a lot of very unhappy people feigning gratitude upon opening their Christmas presents that year.)

To help maintain the mystery of precisely what people are getting for Christmas, presents are traditionally wrapped in paper printed with garish festive designs and tied with a bow. Once people wrapped their gifts in seasonally coloured tissue paper, but in 1917 the US-based company Hallmark Cards produced the first proper wrapping paper as we would know it, after running out of the traditional tissue paper, using decorative envelope linings which they sold for ten cents a sheet.

Since that time the industry has grown almost exponentially and now accounts for around £1.7 billion in retail sales annually. Fifty per cent of all of the paper consumed in the United States is used for gift wrapping, and the general decoration for consumer products, requiring two billion trees to be cut down in the country every year in order to meet the demand. Unfortunately, most of this gift warp ultimately ends up as landfill – four million tons of it!

Did you know...?

The Guinness-recognised World
Record for speedy gift wrapping is
currently held by Hilary Wymer of
the UK. On 9 November 2005, at the
Borders book shop in Manchester
Fort Shopping Park, she wrapped a
Guinness World Records book (aptly
enough) in 19.71 seconds.

Who made the first Christmas cracker?

If there's one thing that helps Christmas go with a bang, it's the traditional Christmas cracker – even if the cracker in question doesn't.

These days, crackers are as traditional as turkey and stuffing although, strangely perhaps, they do not appear during other festivals despite the fact that when they first appeared, they were not restricted to Christmas. As with Christmas cards and Christmas trees, they are a Victorian invention.

It had long been the habit in France of giving children bags of sugared almonds on special occasions. These bags burst with a bang when they were pulled in half. But it wasn't until around the year 1840 that the idea was transported to England.

Thomas Smith, a London baker and confectioner, visited Paris that year and was impressed by the idea of selling bonbons wrapped in twists of paper. If you think about it, the modern cracker – consisting of a cardboard tube wrapped in a brightly decorated piece of paper – looks not unlike an over-sized wrapped sweet. Once back in England, Smith cashed in on the idea himself. When he noticed that young men in particular were buying the twists of sweets for their sweethearts, he began adding love mottoes.

By 1846 he was adding riddles or corny Christmas jokes but when his sweets didn't sell as well as he had hoped he hit on the idea of adding the crack, supposedly after once kicking a log on the fire and hearing it crackle. He experimented with different chemicals to find one which was both safe and easy to make, to make the crack. This was then used to treat a strip of card which was placed inside the newly christened 'cracker', which went on sale in 1847.

It was also the entrepreneurial Smith who added tiny toys, puzzles and games to his crackers. Over the next few years his idea evolved and grew and he moved from his original premises in Clerkenwell, East London, to Finsbury Square. By the end of the nineteenth century the company was producing millions of crackers every year for sale at home and abroad, and is still in business today.

When Thomas Smith died, his sons Tom, Walter and Henry took over the family business. Later Walter erected a drinking fountain in Finsbury Square, in memory of his mother and also to commemorate the life of the man who invented the Christmas cracker. It was Walter who introduced the paper hats. He also toured the world searching out new and unusual ideas for the gifts.

By the turn of the century, Thomas Smith's factory was producing over 13,000,000 crackers every year, which were sold all over the Empire. Incredibly, almost all of the crackers were handmade; the factory machines were only used for assembling the papers for the cracker and making the boxes.

Did you know...?

There is a theory as to why Christmas cracker
jokes are so terrible, and it's all to do with
avoiding familial discord during the festive
season. With your typical joke (such as, 'What do
you get when you cross a joke with a hypothetical
question?') not everyone will find it funny, so if
you tell a good joke you risk dividing the family
into those who liked the joke and those who
didn't, which may result in some of your loved
ones not loving you quite so much anymore.
However, tell a really terrible joke (such as,
'What disease can you get from decorating
your Christmas tree? Tinsellitis') and everyone
is united in hating the joke, and not you, the
wannabe comedian.

The company went on to create special crackers to
honour the Suffragettes, War Heroes, Charlie Chaplin,
The Coronation and many other great occasions. By the
1900s crackers were available in themed packs. There

was even one produced especially for a Leap Year, which included rings and fake marriage certificates for the occasion when a young woman might want to propose to her sweetheart, and suitably expensive 'Millionaire's Crackers' that came with a solid silver box hidden inside, which in turn contained a piece of gold and silver jewellery. They also made exclusive crackers for the Royal Family, Thomas Smith having been granted his first Royal Warrant by the then Prince of Wales in 1906, and still do to this day, although the design and contents are a closely guarded secret.

Pre-war novelty gifts included glass pendants and brooches, bracelets and other jewellery, handmade wooden toys from Norway, musical toys from Germany and solid silver charms, embroidered aprons, handkerchiefs and even jade Buddhas. One famous set of crackers even held a bottle of fine French perfume in each cracker. After the Second World War, however, gifts were kept to a minimum due to lack of money.

Christmas crackers are now all expected to contain three traditional 'surprises': a paper crown, a small gift and a slip of paper bearing a joke or riddle. Although the cracker is a relatively recent invention, the wearing of a hat, or crown, at this particular time of year, dates back thousands of years.

During Roman times, those participating in the annual Saturnalia celebrations wore hats. The specific idea of a paper crown may have arisen from the Twelfth Night celebrations, during which a 'king' or 'queen' was appointed to preside over the proceedings.

Did you know...?

The largest cracker made by the Tom Smith Company was 30 feet, or 9 metres, high! However, the world's longest Christmas cracker was made by the parents of children at Ley Hill School and Pre-School, Chesham, Buckinghamshire, on 20 December 2001. It measured 63.1 m (207 ft) in length, and 4 m (13 ft) in diameter. This monster cracker (made from 200 m of 6" by 2" timber, half a mile of cardboard, 1300 bolts, 1000 nails, 500 screws, half a mile of plastic tape, and constructed over four days) contained 300 balloons, toys, a hat – 2.5 m (8ft) in diameter – and a joke, and was pulled by children of the school and members of Saracens Rugby Club. It even went with a bang.

The largest Christmas cracker pull was achieved by 1,478 participants at the Honda Festival in Tochigi, Japan, on 18 October 2009, whereas the longest Christmas cracker pulling chain consisted of 749 people and was achieved by Brindleyplace in Birmingham, West Midlands, on 11 December 2013. And to finish with a bang, the most Christmas crackers pulled in one minute by a team of two is 52. The record was achieved by Ashrita Furman and Bipin Larkin in New York, USA, on 25 June 2014.

The traditional way to pull a cracker is for everybody sitting at the dinner table to cross their arms and form a circle – gripping their own cracker in their right hand while taking hold of their neighbour's with their left – so that everyone's cracker is pulled at the same time.

The A to Z of Christmas

is for Queen's Speech

The Queen's speech is as much a part of Christmas as over-eating and spending far too much money on presents. And yet it is also one of the more recently developed popular Christmas traditions.

The practice of the monarch making a speech to the nation was begun in 1932, when King George V (father of our own monarch) broadcast a Christmas message to the British people over the radio. His speech was transmitted live from his small study at Sandringham, in Norfolk, where the royal family always spend their Christmas holidays together.

He began with the words, 'I speak now from my home and from my heart to you all'. However, King George wasn't reading his own words. The speech had been written for him by Rudyard Kipling who is much better known as the author of *The Jungle Book* and the *Just So Stories*

On Christmas Day 1952, on the occasion of her first Christmas message to the Commonwealth, our own Queen Elizabeth II began:

> Each Christmas, at this time, my beloved father broadcast a message to his people in all parts of the world... As he used to do, I am speaking to you from my own home, where I am spending Christmas with my family.

From 1957 onwards, the Queen's speech transferred to television. The speech is filmed in the week before Christmas at Windsor Castle, and pieced together from multiple takes, as planes flying in and out of Heathrow airport regularly disrupt the recording. It is sent to seventeen Commonwealth countries around the world, to be broadcast at a convenient local time, which, in the UK, is always 3 p.m., Christmas Day.

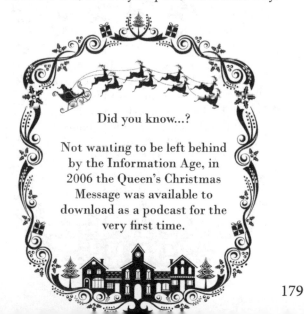

Did you know...?

Not wanting to be left behind by the Information Age, in 2006 the Queen's Christmas Message was available to download as a podcast for the very first time.

In her famous 1992 '*annus horribilus*' speech, the Queen expressed the sorrow she felt at the end of a year which has seen the break-up of two family marriages, one divorce and a catastrophic fire at Windsor Castle.

Ever since 1993, Channel 4 have broadcast their own 'alternative' Christmas message at the same time as the Queen's. The first of these iconoclastic speakers was the author and gay icon, Quentin Crisp. Other speakers have covered the whole gamut of British characters from the likes of Doreen and Neville Lawrence, parents of the murdered schoolboy Stephen Lawrence, to the spoof comedy character Ali G, and even the fictional Marge Simpson.

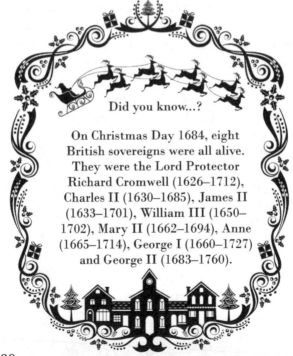

Did you know...?

On Christmas Day 1684, eight British sovereigns were all alive. They were the Lord Protector Richard Cromwell (1626–1712), Charles II (1630–1685), James II (1633–1701), William III (1650–1702), Mary II (1662–1694), Anne (1665–1714), George I (1660–1727) and George II (1683–1760).

As well as the Queen's speech, what would Christmas Day be without the big Christmas Day movie? In 2013, Total Film magazine published its list of the Top Ten Christmas Movies. Some of them might seem like rather strange choices for a list of festive films, but each and every one takes place around Christmas time, even if they don't all have a particularly festive theme.

It's A Wonderful Life (1946)

Die Hard (1988)

Elf (2003)

Gremlins (1984)

The Nightmare Before Christmas (1993)

The Muppet Christmas Carol (1992)

Home Alone (1990)

Miracle On 34th Street (1947)

Scrooged (1988)

Bad Santa (2003)

Why are sprouts eaten with Christmas dinner?

Picture the scene. You sit down to dinner on Christmas Day, looking forward to tucking into turkey with all the trimmings, your plate is piled high with roast potatoes, parsnips, sausages wrapped in bacon, all smothered with gravy, and then the lurid green balls of bitterness hove into view. Brussels sprouts.

Children hate them, as do most adults, and yet you have to have them as part of your otherwise utterly delicious Christmas dinner. And why? Because they're traditional! And besides, you've no doubt been told that they're good for you too.

But whose fault is it that you have to sit through the most magnificent meal of the year dreading the fact that at some point you're going to have to pop one of those malodorous mini cabbages into your mouth?

Did you know...?

According to one survey carried out in 2002, Brussels sprouts were the most hated vegetable in Britain.

Brussels sprouts are unusual in that they are one of the few vegetables to have originated in Northern Europe. They are members of the *Brassica* family (which also includes cabbages, cauliflowers, broccoli and kale), cultivated first from the wild cabbage. They also just happen to come into season during the winter and are supposedly best harvested later on in the season, after they have suffered a few sharp frosts. In times gone by, the only fresh vegetables you could eat during the winter were those which were in season at that time of year, and sprouts fitted the bill at Christmas time.

But what has Brussels, capital of Belgium and the European Union, got to do with sprouts? Well, the first written reference to Brussels sprouts comes from 1587. They became known as Brussels sprouts because it is believed that they were widely cultivated in that part of Belgium in the sixteenth century.

When it comes to cooking them, it is common practice to cut them with a cross on their base. Most cooks who carry out this practice, before dropping the sprouts into boiling water, will tell you they do so to ensure that the inside will cook at the same rate as the outside. However, current culinary thinking has it that crossing the sprout in this way results in a loss of flavour.

However, there is another reason why they are crossed, and that, like so many Christmas traditions, is based on good old-fashioned paranoid superstition. It is supposed to keep the Devil out (but as far as this writer's concerned, the Devil's welcome to them).

If you've ever wondered why sprouts are so blighted with 'a powerful smell of drains', as the Victorians euphemistically put it, it's all down to chemistry. During cooking, sprouts release sulphur compounds which have that all-too-familiar and none-too-pleasant smell of rotten eggs. However, they can smell even worse *after* they've been eaten! These same chemical compounds react with bacteria in the gut to produce hydrogen sulphide, which is the constituent ingredient of stink bombs.

Did you know...?

In 2007, gastro-genius Heston Blumenthal created a Christmas meal like no other for six celebrity diners: actor Richard E. Grant, comedians Rob Brydon, Sue Perkins and Dara O'Briain, journalist Kirsty Wark and broadcaster Terry Wogan. The meal went as follows:

Mulled wine

Hot on one side of the glass, cold on the other

Edible baubles

Made of blown sugar, filled with smoked salmon mousse

Gold, frankincense and myrrh

Langoustine, onion and vermouth stock cubes, wrapped in edible gold leaf and dissolved in frankincense water, served with a carved myrrh-wood spoon

Babe in a manger

Communion wafer sprayed with the aroma of freshly washed baby

Flaming whiskey sorbet

Scented with the perfume of a wood-panelled room, complete with roaring fire and leather armchair

Hand-reared roast goose

Goose fed on apple powder, Paxo stuffing and essential oil of Christmas tree, accompanied by sherbet fountains made from the powdered goose feed with vanilla straws

Pommes purées with goose, chestnut and bacon velouté

Served in a bell jar containing the smoky aroma of roasted chestnuts

Reindeer milk ice cream

Frozen in liquid nitrogen

185

Other than that rather nasty aromatic side effect, it's no wonder that children don't like sprouts. Your taste buds develop as you grow older and, as a result, sprouts really are more distasteful to children than they are to adults, as sensitivity to tastes tends to decrease as you get older. There's a perfectly acceptable scientific reason why the little green devils taste so bad; their bitter taste is a chemical defence evolved by the *brassica oleracea* to stop insects from attacking it.

So yes, sprouts *are* traditional – having arisen out of a traditional necessity to eat during the cold winter months – and what's more, they're good for you too.

Brussels sprouts, like cabbages, are members of the cruciferous family of vegetables, which are a good source of the antioxidant vitamins A and C, potassium and iron. They also contain something called sinigrin, which may, according to some sources, help to prevent bowel cancer. Good news for sprout farmers and those keen on keeping healthy but bad news for anyone who doesn't like eating their greens as to gain their full benefit you have to eat about 10 oz (280 g) of sprouts a day.

Why do people go to pantomimes during the Christmas season?

Everyone loves a traditional pantomime, don't they?

Oh no they don't!

Oh yes they do!

Like so much else that is to do with the season of peace and goodwill, pantomime has its origins in the distant past. In this case it was the Ancient Greeks who were enjoying pantomime performances long before it was ever heard of in this country.

'Pantomime' comes from two Greek words, *panto* meaning 'all' and *mimos*, meaning 'mimic'. The *pantomimos* was originally a solo dancer who played all the parts, accompanied by a sung narrative or music played on a flute. In time the name for the dancer came to apply to the performance itself.

Two familiar aspects of the modern pantomime are the reversal of fortunes – Cinderella marries her prince while poor Jack makes a million – and the flexible nature of traditional gender roles; a man dresses in drag to play the part of the dame, while the principal boy is always a girl! The Celtic Samhain (the predecessor of Halloween) was also a time of chaos in which the normal order was reversed, and so also had its part to play in the development of the Christmas panto. One of the traditional figures of Samhain was the She-Male, a bearded lady, or rather a bearded man wearing a dress. By the Middle Ages, this deliberate confusing of the gender roles had become part of the Twelfth Night celebrations, which were a combination of the feast of Epiphany and the older midwinter feast.

But before there was pantomime as we know it in England, there were the mystery and miracle plays. During the Medieval period, mystery plays (in which the performers acted out stories from the Bible) and miracle plays (which specifically re-enacted episodes from the lives of the saints), were one of the most

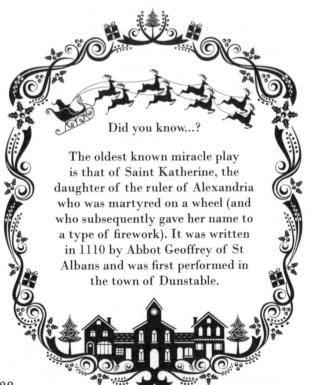

Did you know...?

The oldest known miracle play is that of Saint Katherine, the daughter of the ruler of Alexandria who was martyred on a wheel (and who subsequently gave her name to a type of firework). It was written in 1110 by Abbot Geoffrey of St Albans and was first performed in the town of Dunstable.

popular forms of Christmas entertainment. This form of theatre grew out of a type of religious drama, which itself appeared in the tenth and eleventh centuries, and which was designed to help the illiterate layman learn his Bible.

As mystery and miracle plays grew in popularity they ended up encompassing the whole Bible, with re-enactments of the Creation to Christ's crucifixion and his subsequent resurrection. Some even included Doomsday – a pre-enactment, if you like.

These plays were parts of cycles and would be performed over an entire day, either close to Christmas or in the lead up to Easter. Having grown out of a form of liturgical theatre, in which monks played all the parts, these plays were performed outside churches with huge crowds of onlookers.

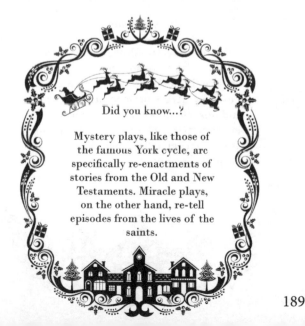

Did you know...?

Mystery plays, like those of the famous York cycle, are specifically re-enactments of stories from the Old and New Testaments. Miracle plays, on the other hand, re-tell episodes from the lives of the saints.

However, after Pope Innocent III forbade clergy to act in public, in 1210, secular actors took over the putting on of the plays and, under the influence of a secular voice, they quickly became ruder and even lewder. As a result, they were soon considered inappropriate for a church audience and so transferred to the town streets.

With the plays' move to the towns, the guilds became involved, taking over the organisation of performances. However, despite this added level of authentication,

Did you know...?

To our understanding, a pageant is a play or procession, but the name originally described a portable stage used by actors performing mystery and miracle plays. These wagons were constructed with two tiers of staging on top of them. This meant they could be pulled to any given venue, usually outside the house of someone wealthy enough to pay for the privilege.

the actors themselves were seen as little better than beggars and vagabonds, and were considered to be on the bottom rung of the social ladder.

Did you know...?

The animal masks of the Medieval mummers have survived to make it into the modern panto in the form of the animal-costume roles of Daisy the Cow and the traditional pantomime horse.

This experience of theatre would not have been what many were used to. In Medieval times, the majority of the population still lived in the countryside and so, unless they happened to visit a town where a mystery cycle was being performed, the common man wouldn't have been exposed to such entertainment.

The form of theatre the common man would have been most familiar with was that performed by mummers. The words 'mummer' and 'mumming' (the ancient form of street theatre they revelled in) either come from the German *mumme*, meaning a 'mask' or 'masker', or the Greek *momme*, meaning specifically 'a frightening mask', and so is realistically a combination of both.

The possible origins of their name give an insight into the nature of the mummers' performance. An important aspect of mumming was that performers disguised themselves by wearing masks, often in the form of animal heads. And if not masks, then their faces were blackened and they wore hooded robes of rags and ribbons instead. It was believed that if a mummer was recognised then the magic spell that the players cast would be broken.

Thousands of years ago, long before the rise of Christianity, mumming wasn't a theatrical performance at all but a fertility rite that acknowledged the death of the year in the depths of winter, and its subsequent rebirth with the coming of spring. If any of those carrying out this rite were recognised, the ritual could fail and the summer would never return at all.

However, by the Middle Ages, the true purpose of the mummers' plays had become obscured by the Christianising of the old midwinter festivals. The recurring cast of characters now included such larger-than-life characters as Beelzebub, Father Christmas (sometimes carrying a club in his guise as Old Man Winter), Saint George, the dragon he slew or alternatively the Turkish Knight, and the King of Egypt. Often there was an Old Dame, who was George's mother, and a Doctor who was able to miraculously bring our hero back to life after he had been slain by his enemy, whether dragon or Saracen.

It is likely that the killing of the hero and his subsequent resurrection at the hands of the doctor was a hangover from the original fertility rite through which mumming developed, symbolising winter killing the crops which spring then brings back to life.

This story of heroic combat was the most common subject matter of mummers' plays and featured a ritualised sword fight. The words spoken by the actors were frequently crude rhyming couplets and often made little sense.

The Medieval mummers' plays reached their height in the fifteenth century, but by the sixteenth century their popularity was waning again, with the establishment of more developed theatre from Europe. Modern pantomime has much in common, in terms of style and content, with the *commedia dell'arte*, a form of improvised theatre that arose in Italy in the Middle Ages. Recurring characters from plays in this tradition were the lovers, the father and servants and are still found in modern pantomimes today, such as Cinderella.

In seventeenth century England, pantomime was seen as being a low form of opera. It continued to develop, however, and by the eighteenth century pantomimes had become much more topical as well as comical, under such pioneers as the actor-manager John Rich of London. It is the popular belief that one of the first theatres to stage what someone in the twenty-first century would recognise as something akin to a proper pantomime was the Drury Lane Theatre. Augustus Harris, the manager of Drury Lane during the 1870s, is now considered the father of modern pantomime as a result.

Throughout the eighteenth and nineteenth centuries the traditional characters and plots of the *commedia dell'arte* were mixed up with fairy tales, folk legends, and even stories from the *Arabian Nights*, until this form of theatre ended up with its dozen or so stock stories.

Did you know...?

In the tradition of *commedia dell'arte*, the right-hand side of the stage symbolised Heaven while the left side represented Hell. One of the rules that modern panto should still adhere to is that the good character (such as the fairy godmother) always enters from the right while the villain (such as the magician Abanazar) enters from the left.

194

And of course audience participation is the name of the game in the modern panto.

Oh no, it isn't!

Oh yes, it is!

It is probably the only form of theatre where the paying audience have to work almost as hard as the actors they're paying to see.

Boooooo! Hissss!

He's behind you!

───── **The A to Z of Christmas** ─────

ℝ

is for Roland le Pettour

Today we think of a minstrel as being someone who makes a living from singing songs whilst accompanying themselves on the guitar, or maybe the lute (if you're more Medievally-minded). However, in Medieval times, a minstrel was more like a cross between a musician and a stand-up comedian (someone rather like Bill Bailey). As one thirteenth century poem put it, a true minstrel was someone who could:

> Speak and rhyme well, be witty, know the story of Troy, balance apples on the point of knives, juggle, jump through hoops, play the citole, mandora, harp, fiddle, and psaltery.

The same poem goes on to offer further useful advice for securing gainful employment as a minstrel, including learning how to do bird imitations, performing with dogs and donkeys, and being a skilled puppeteer.

The aforementioned sword juggling was a skill possessed by the dwarf Taillefer, one of two jesters (the

Did you know...?

Another popular act, at least among the English royalty during the Medieval period, involved the minstrel spreading honey on something you normally wouldn't even think of spreading honey on, before a performing bear was brought in to the feast hall. Apparently it was rather like the putting-your-head-in-the-lion's-mouth trick, only the trick didn't involve the minstrel putting his head anywhere near a lion's mouth, which might almost have been preferable, when you think about it.

other being Turold), named on the Bayeux Tapestry as being present at the Battle of Hastings. Taillefer rode out before the discouraged Norman army and, "tossed his sword high and sported with it". When one of the English emerged from his battle-line to laugh at him, Taillefer promptly cut the man's head off. Unsurprisingly, this encouraged the Norman army, who of course went on to win the battle.

But what do juggling dwarfs, minstrels, and English royalty have to do with Roland le Pettour? And what did he do that was deserving of the rich reward of thirty acres of land?

Roland was court jester to Henry II and as part of the Christmas festivities at court, he performed, as the Latin scholars would have it, *"unum saltum et siffletum et unum bumbulum"* – or to put it in the vulgar tongue, "a jump, a whistle, and a fart". Roland's musical abilities went so far as being able to fart tunes, and the king found this so amusing that he granted the Medieval flatulist the manor of Hemingstone in Suffolk, in return for his very particular 'services'. The land was passed down from father to son for many generations, on one condition – that the current incumbent appear at court each Christmas Day to perform the same leap, whistle and fart, that Roland had made so popular.

Roland the Farter has become a legend in his own right, thanks to his unusual party piece, to the point where the templar-metal band Jaldaboath wrote their own tune in celebration of his achievements for their 2014 album 'The Further Adventures...' It is as crude and as vulgar as Roland's act undoubtedly was.

What is wassailing?

Here we come a-wassailing
Among the leaves so green,
Here we come a-wandering,
So fair to be seen:
Love and joy come to you,
And to you your wassail too,
And God bless you, and send you
A happy New Year,
And God send you
A happy New Year.

Wassailing used to be a popular part of the Christmas festivities in England and the memory of it still lingers in the words of certain carols, but what was wassailing, and how exactly did people go about it?

Wassail itself was a hot drink which pre-dates the Christian festival by some centuries. The word 'wassail' comes from the Old English *wæs hæl* which literally meant 'be whole' and so, by extension, 'be healthy'. The phrase 'hale and hearty' has its origins in this expression as well.

The ceremony from which wassailing developed was a toast to the sun as it rose on the morning after the shortest day of the winter solstice. It, like the veneration of evergreens, was believed to encourage a bountiful harvest (specifically that of fruit) in the year to come.

The transformation of the winter festival to a

Christian one did nothing to diminish the popularity of the wassail toast and it persisted, like so much else, becoming interwoven with the newer Christianised celebrations.

Did you know...?

The expression 'to drink a toast' actually has its origins in the wassail. By the time the practice of wassailing had left the lord's manor, with bands of peasants taking their empty wassail bowl from house to house for it to be filled with drink, the wassailers were sometimes given pieces of toast – rather like croutons – to float on the top. Each wassailer in turn took a piece and wished his fellows good cheer before eating the toast and washing it down with a swig of the potent mixture in the bowl. Hence the phrase 'to drink a toast'.

In Saxon England, at the start of the year, the lord of the manor would shout the greeting *wæs hæl* to his assembled household who would respond with the words *drinc hæl*, meaning 'drink and be healthy'. His lordship would then take a swig from a large wooden bowl – the Wassail Bowl or Wassail Cup – before passing it on to the next most senior member of the household. And so it would be passed down the line until everyone had had a drink.

The fact that a drink whose constituent ingredient is ale should be called wassail is purely a coincidence. Apples are an important component of the recipe, along with spices and sugar, which was added late in the drink's development when it became more widely available.

Wassail

6 cups of ale

1 cup of sugar

Pinch of cinnamon

Pinch of ginger

Pinch of cloves

Pinch of nutmeg

6 beaten eggs

4 roasted apples

Heat the ale in a saucepan, add the sugar and spices and bring almost to the boil. Take it off the heat and gradually add a little of the hot mixture to the beaten eggs. Return it to the saucepan and cook, this time stirring constantly until the mixture has thickened slightly. Put the roasted apples in a punch bowl (which must be heat-proof) and pour the mixture over them.

Due to its unusual mix of ingredients – which could include whipping cream instead of eggs – the contents of the Wassail Cup often had a frothy, foamy appearance. This gave the wassail drink its other name of 'lamb's wooll'. Here is a variation on the wassail recipe which goes by that name.

Lamb's Wooll

6 bottles of brown ale

1 cup of sherry

450 g/1lb light brown sugar

2 roasted apples, sliced

1 lemon, sliced

½ tsp ginger

½ tsp cinnamon

½ a nutmeg

2 slices of toasted white bread

Heat one bottle of ale. Put the sugar in a

large heat-proof bowl and stir well. Grate the half a nutmeg into the sugar-ale mixture, add cinnamon and ginger, then the sherry and the rest of the ale. Leave to stand for several hours. Before serving, finish it off with the sliced lemon and apples and float pieces of the toasted bread on top.

As an alternative to the traditional ale-based wassail or lamb's wooll, you might want to try this West Country recipe for mulled cider.

Mulled Cider

1 litre/2 pints of still cider

2 small eating apples

4 cloves

140 ml/¼ pint of water

50 g/2 oz soft brown sugar

1 cinnamon stick

1 tsp ground ginger

2 tangerines

Stick the apples with two of the cloves each and then bake. Heat the cider and, at the same time, heat the other ingredients (minus the orange) until all the sugar has dissolved, and then simmer for 5 minutes. Place the baked apples and tangerine pieces in a heat-proof punch bowl, strain the spiced water into it and lastly add the hot cider.

If you have children among your household who would like to partake of the wassail, or you need to keep a clear head yourself (perhaps it's your turn to be the designated Christmas driver), then why not try this alcohol-free version?

A Teetotal Wassail

3 litres/6 pints of apple juice

1½ litres/3 pints of peach juice

½ cup of freshly-squeezed lemon juice

1 large orange

Cloves

6 cinnamon sticks

Stick the orange with whole cloves (roughly half an inch apart) and bake it in the oven. After half an hour take it out and puncture it in several places with a fork. Place the orange with the other ingredients in a large pot and cover. Bring the mixture to the boil before simmering for half an hour. Pour the hot mixture into your heat-proof punch bowl, adding the orange and cinnamon sticks. (This recipe makes around 30 servings!)

As time went on, the alcoholic element of the wassail took over in popularity, with the ceremony eventually being absorbed into the general eat, drink and be merry ethos of the raucous celebrations.

By Tudor times, wassailing peasants had become a menace, with the drunken common folk weaving their way from the home of one rich landowner to another, singing carols (with all the tunefulness of a drunk) and refusing to leave until they were paid off with an appropriate gift, or sometimes just hard cash.

In the traditional wassailers' chant 'We Wish you a Merry Christmas', the revellers demand food, in the form of figgy pudding. The words of the carol include the veiled threat of 'We won't go until we get some!' However, in the words of the Gloucestershire Wassail, the threat of physical violence is made perfectly plain:

> Come butler, come fill us a bowl of the best
> Then we hope that your soul in heaven may rest
> But if you do draw us a bowl of the small
> Then down shall go butler, bowl and all.

Just as the original pagan wassail ceremony was intended to encourage a bountiful harvest of fruit in the year to come, it was also at Christmas time that wassailers would bless the apple orchards. This practice was most prevalent in the fruit-growing counties of Kent and the West of England, and took place on Twelfth Night.

In this case it was often cider that filled the Wassail Cup and, having drunk of it themselves, the orchard owners would water the roots of the fruit trees with it, in the hope that it would ensure the plants' fertility for the year to come. They would then make as much noise as possible to drive away evil spirits before heading home to get back to the serious business of drinking. In more modern times, in some areas, men would then discharge their shotguns into the branches of the trees, while in Surrey the trunks were whipped!

The practice of wassailing did eventually lose favour, when the Puritans tried to get rid of Christmas for good. It was the Victorians who really revived the custom but in the process they converted it into the practice of carolling from door to door that is now so popular.

And so, it can be seen that wassail, originally a drink, came to mean the ceremony of which it was an integral part, and from there the song, sung with ale-inspired enthusiasm.

The wooden Wassail Bowl, or Cup, steadily took on greater and greater significance throughout the Medieval period, being decorated with ribbons and greenery. In some parts of England, New Year was celebrated with a wassailing procession. Two young girls bearing the Wassail Bowl between them would lead the procession from house to house, inviting those they visited to partake of the contents of the cup before re-filling it with their own supply of alcohol.

> Our wassail cup is made of the rosemary tree,
> And so is your beer of the best barley.
> Call up the butler of this house
> Put on his golden ring;

Let him bring us up a glass of beer,
And better we shall sing.

The A to Z of Christmas

is for Snapdragon

Snapdragon was a popular parlour game from the sixteenth to nineteenth centuries. It was played during the winter, particularly on Christmas Eve or Twelfth Night. Brandy was heated and placed in a wide shallow bowl, before raisins were added and the whole lot set alight. The aim of the game was to pluck the raisins out of the burning brandy and eat them, at the risk of being burnt.

Other treats could also be used. Of these almonds were the most common alternative or addition, but currants, candied fruit, figs, grapes, and plums also featured. Salt could also be sprinkled in the bowl. In one variation a Christmas pudding is placed in the centre of the bowl with raisins around it.

In *The Winter's Tale*, Shakespeare used the word 'snapdragon' as a verb, to describe a moment when a ship at sea is instantly swallowed up by a storm, just as the raisins are gobbled up by those playing the game.

Snapdragon is also mentioned in Lewis Carroll's

Through the Looking-Glass, and What Alice Found There, when the eponymous heroine meets the peculiar Looking-Glass insects. One of them is the Snap-dragon-fly, with a body made of plum-pudding, its wings of holly leaves and its head a raisin burning in brandy. It lives on frumenty and mince pies, and nests in a Christmas box.

Who was Good King Wenceslas?

A popular carol sung each Christmas is 'Good King Wenceslas'. Traditionally reserved for the Feast of Saint Stephen's Day (26 December) it tells the story of the aforementioned good king looking out of his castle to see a poor man foraging for firewood in the forest. In an act of Christian charity, Wenceslas decides to spread the Christmas cheer and sets off with his page, into the cold and the dark, to make sure that the wretch enjoys himself to the full. But who was the real life inspiration for the saintly monarch, and was good King Wenceslas as good as the carol would have us believe?

Well, first of all you can discard the narrative from the carol as fact, as it was invented by that infamous Victorian caroller, J.M. Neale in 1853. Neale was the translator of both the Advent hymn 'O come, O come, Emmanuel' and the popular carol 'Good Christian Men Rejoice'. When it came to 'Good King Wenceslas', he took what was originally the tune of a springtime carol, *'Tempus adest floridum'*, to provide his saccharin-sweet festive number with a melody.

You'll be relieved to hear that Wenceslas did at least exist, although he wasn't a king. He was actually a duke, but you could call him a prince if you were feeling generous. Born circa AD 907, in Stochov near Prague, in what is now the Czech Republic, he was ruler of the principality of Bohemia. He was raised as a Christian by his grandmother Saint Ludmilla. His mother, Drahomíra, was a pagan, and ruthlessly ambitious. She had Ludmilla murdered and then ruled as regent herself until Wenceslas came of age. However, intrigue plagued her court and a desire on the behalf of the populace of Bohemia to see an end to the conflicts between the Christian and non-Christian factions within the region led to Wenceslas taking the reins of government himself.

As a mark of his pious Christian upbringing, it is said that Wenceslas took a vow of virginity and that German missionary priests, seeking to make Bohemia Christian, enjoyed his wholehearted support. By 929, Christianity was spreading throughout Bohemia, but Wenceslas' own converting zeal upset his non-Christian rivals. That same year, faced with the threat of invasions from Germany, Wenceslas submitted to the German king, Henry I. This upset the nobles still further who then plotted to get rid of him. These same nobles colluded with Wenceslas' own brother, Boleslav, who then waylaid him on the way to mass. Boleslav cut him down at the door to the church, hacking him to pieces. Wenceslas was only 22 years old.

Almost as soon as he was buried, there came

reports of miracles taking place at Wenceslas' tomb. In 932, fearful of reprisals from beyond the grave, the superstitious Boleslav had his dead brother's remains disinterred and moved to the church of Saint Vitus, in Prague itself. The church was a popular pilgrimage site during Medieval times and eventually became a cathedral. Wenceslas himself was canonised and made patron saint of Bohemia.

When, and why, was Christmas cancelled?

There is a classic, melodramatic line in the movie *Robin Hood, Prince of Thieves* when an enraged Sheriff of Nottingham (played by Alan Rickman, hamming it up to within an inch of his life) declares, in a moment of moustache-twirling villainy, 'Cancel the kitchen scraps for lepers and orphans, no more merciful beheadings, and call off Christmas!'

What many people don't know is that Christmas *was* cancelled, for real, but it wasn't in the twelfth or thirteenth century. It was in fact in the seventeenth century.

During the 1640s and '50s it was against the law to celebrate Christmas, with various pieces of legislation put in place making it illegal for churches to open on Christmas Day (unless it was a Sunday of course), for mince pies to be eaten and for people to decorate their houses with holly, ivy and mistletoe. Many people have blamed the Lord Protector of England at this time, the king-killer Oliver Cromwell, for this cessation of festive fun, but in reality it was just part of the seventeenth century Puritan crackdown on fun and frivolity in general.

From the late sixteenth century onwards, many pious people had come to frown upon the pagan-themed Christmas celebrations; they disliked the extravagance, waste, disorder, sin and immorality to which it inevitably led, and they saw it as a link back to Roman Catholicism – it was called Christ's Mass after all (mass being a specifically Catholic ceremony).The Puritans argued that there was nothing in the Bible that said God wanted the faithful to mark Christ's birth in any special way. And it wasn't only Christmas they wanted to get rid of. They had it in for Easter and Whitsun as well.

In the early 1640s, the Long Parliament had already begun to clamp down on Christmas, even changing its name to 'Christ-tide', so as to distance themselves from the feast day's Catholic connections. Parliament said that if Christ-tide was to be kept at all, it should be as a day of fasting and prayer. It was business as usual when the Long Parliament convened on 25 December 1643. In 1644, parliament stressed that 25 December was to be kept as a time of fasting and humiliation, when the faithful should think on the sins of those who had turned the day into a feast in the past. Both Houses of Parliament attended intense fast sermons on 25 December 1644.

That year Cromwell's administration passed an Act of Parliament that banned any form of celebration during the Twelve Days of Christmas. Their excuse for passing such an Act was that there was no mention of Christmas in the Bible and so it was deemed to be ungodly.

However, strict Puritans took the greatest exception to the pagan elements which made up the Christmas festivities which, let's face it, was most of them. Christmas Day itself was dubbed 'Satan's working day' by the more extreme members of the Puritan cause, or even the 'Antichrist's Mass'. They particularly loathed the idea of wassailing – the practice of going door-to-door carol-singing in return for booze – which more often than not ended up as an out of control drunken revel.

In January 1645 parliament produced a new Directory of Public Worship which made it clear that Sundays were to be strictly observed as holy days, for the worship of God, and that there were to be no other, 'festival days, vulgarly called Holy Days'. Accompanying legislation made it illegal for any other forms of worship or church services to take place, especially Christmas. In June 1647 the Long Parliament passed an Ordinance making it absolutely clear that the feasts of Christmas, Easter and Whitsun were abolished.

During the 1650s further laws were passed. Christmas carols were banned, shops and markets were ordered to stay open on 25 December, and those found holding or attending a special Christmas church service could be fined or put in the stocks – whether they were men, women or children. In London, soldiers were ordered to patrol the streets and take any food suspected of being cooked for an illicit Christmas celebration, by force if necessary. Nativity scenes were banned as the worship of idols, and the use of the word Christmas itself, was seen as taking the Lord's name in vain.

25 December became a typically dreary day of everyday work and fasting. For eighteen barren years Britain was officially a country without Christmas. However, although Christmas celebrations were banned, they did not die out. Instead they went

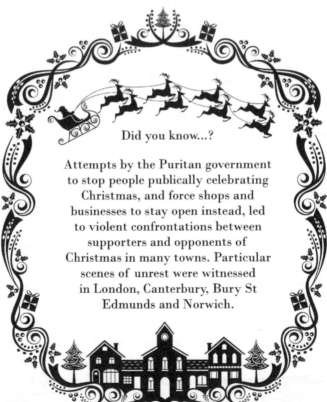

Did you know...?

Attempts by the Puritan government to stop people publically celebrating Christmas, and force shops and businesses to stay open instead, led to violent confrontations between supporters and opponents of Christmas in many towns. Particular scenes of unrest were witnessed in London, Canterbury, Bury St Edmunds and Norwich.

underground until 1660. Despite the risks, people held secretive religious services marking Christ's birth and also maintained the secular aspects of the day.

With the Restoration of the monarchy in 1660, when Charles II took the throne of England, the Directory of Public Worship and all other anti-Christmas legislation brought in from 1642–60 was declared null and void, and done away with. There are some historians who believe that the common man's desire to see the traditional, raucous Christmas celebrations restored helped lead to the Restoration of the monarchy!

However, after eighteen years without a publically recognised Christmas, the nation did not immediately resume the traditional feasting and other celebrations. Enter William Winstanley, an Essex farmer's son, diarist and writer, and the man who saved Christmas.

Under the pen-name of Poor Robin Goodfellow, Winstanley extolled the joys of Christmas. He believed that Christmas was a time for helping those worse off than oneself and, if it was celebrated properly, that it gave the poor and the destitute something to look forward to as the cold, dark days of winter drew on.

Winstanley lobbied powerful lords – and even the King himself – to set an example to others by opening their houses, so that family, friends and tenants might partake of feasting and other entertainments. He encouraged carol-singing once again, with carols such as 'God Rest Ye Merry Gentlemen' and 'I Saw Three Ships' being particular favourites, and dancing too, 'the whole company, young and old, footing it lustily to the merry sound of the pipe and fiddle'.

is for Tinsel

What would the traditional Christmas tree be like without its boughs decked with strings of shredded metal foil? For some, the appeal of tinsel is the way it mimics the sparkling effect of icicles (particularly the long narrow strips known as 'lametta'). For others, it's the way it spreads the glow of fairy lights into every corner of a room.

The name may come from the Old French word *estincele*, which translates as 'sparkle', but tinsel is in fact another of the gifts that has been bequeathed to the rest of the world by the Germans. The first tinsel was made in Nuremberg in 1610, from extruded strips of silver, or shredded gold foil. Despite being a durable metal, silver tarnishes quickly, particularly in candlelight, and the blackened tinsels that resulted were not a pretty sight, necessitating the need to find a suitable substitute.

A mixture of lead and tin was tried, but the mixture proved to be awfully heavy, even breaking down under its own weight. The inexorable march

Did you know...?

Tinsel has many traditional uses in India, including decorations on images, garlands for weddings and other ceremonies, and even ornamental trappings for horses and elephants. It is also used at Christmas, despite the fact that the population of India are predominantly Hindu, Muslim and Buddhist. Christians in India decorate mango and banana trees at Christmas time, rather than conifers, and they also decorate their houses with mango leaves (the plant taking the place of evergreens). In some parts of India, small oil-burning lamps are used as Christmas decorations. They are placed on the edges of flat roofs and on the tops of walls, while churches are decorated with poinsettias and lit with candles for the Christmas Eve service.

of the Industrial Age meant that by the twentieth century manufacturing advances allowed for the production of cheap aluminium-based tinsel, with the world leader in this area being France.

Production had to be curtailed during the First World War as a result of the demand for copper for the war effort. However, by the 1950s, long after the Second World War, tinsel and tinsel garlands were so popular that they became more commonly used than Christmas lights, tinsel being much less of a fire hazard (the then-popular artificial Christmas trees being made out of flammable aluminized paper!).

Today, most tinsel isn't made from costly metals at all. It is actually made from plastic, specifically polyvinyl chloride film, coated with a metallic finish.

What does the humble robin have to do with Christmas?

The robin, with its bright red breast plumage, is a familiar image of the festive season, usually depicted on Christmas cards amid a thicket of ivy or hopping about in the snow. But why, of all birds, has the robin become so associated with the midwinter festival?

This familiar British bird should really be called the European robin (as opposed to the American robin, Australasian robin, Pekin robin or Japanese hill robin) or, to give the British subspecies its full Latin name *Erithacus rubecula melophilus*. Robins are insectivorous and sing a fluting, warbling song. This is heard during the breeding season, when the birds can sing into the evening, and even on into the night.

The bird has become known as the gardener's friend because it is relatively unafraid of humans and so will come close to anyone digging in soil, on the lookout for earthworms and other food turned up by the spade. Robins are still active in winter and stand out in the snow with their rufous feathers as they hunt for grubs.

It is possible that the link with Christmas comes from another Viking connection. In Norse mythology, the robin was believed to be a storm-cloud bird and so was sacred to Thor, god of thunder. (And of course Thor had his own part to play in the development of the Father Christmas myth, riding across the sky as he did in his goat-drawn iron chariot.)

The association with Christmas more probably arises, however, from the fact that postmen in Victorian Britain wore red uniforms and were nicknamed 'Robins' as a result. Their uniforms were red because they worked for the Royal Mail and red was considered a royal colour. The robin that appears on Christmas cards is really an emblem of the postman delivering the card.

As to why robins appear so frequently on Christmas cards, it is in part because the British are a nation of bird-lovers and the robin is one of the most – if not *the* most – attractive and colourful birds that can be seen in gardens and hedgerows throughout the winter season.

There is one legend in particular that strengthens the

robin's connection with Christmas. The tale goes that after Jesus was born, Joseph had to go out to collect wood to feed the fire that was keeping the infant Christ warm. He was gone for such a long time that Mary began to worry, convinced that the fire would go out before he returned.

At that moment a flock of small brown birds flew down and landed beside the dying fire. By flapping their wings they fanned the embers and in this way were able to keep the fire alight until Joseph returned with more fuel. But their selfless act had not been without cost to the poor birds. Mary saw that they had scorched their breast feathers in their efforts to keep the fire alight.

Addressing the birds Mary declared that, 'From now on you will always have a fiery red breast in memory of what you have done for the baby Jesus. People will love you and will call you Robin Redbreast'.

Having been there at his birth, there is another Christian legend that places the robin at the scene of Christ's death as well. As Jesus made his way to the hill of Calvary, dragging the cross on which he was to be executed, the crown of thorns that the Roman soldiers had placed on his head, mockingly calling Him 'King of the Jews', dug into his flesh, tearing the skin and adding to his pain.

One thorn was more deeply embedded than all the others. As Jesus went on his way, a plain brown bird flew down onto his head and tried to pull the thorn free with its beak. At last, thanks to a great amount of effort on the bird's part, the snagged thorn came free and with it, a drop of Christ's blood. The blood splashed onto the bird's breast, staining it bright red, and so the robin gained its distinctive ruddy plumage.

And there is one more story that connects the robin to the festival of Christ's Mass. This one takes place after Christ's death, when his uncle, Joseph of Arimathea, travelled to England. According to this particular legend, the robin came with him, and its offspring were born with red breasts as a reminder of how Joseph of Arimathea had given up his tomb for Christ to be interred within, his greatest act of kindness.

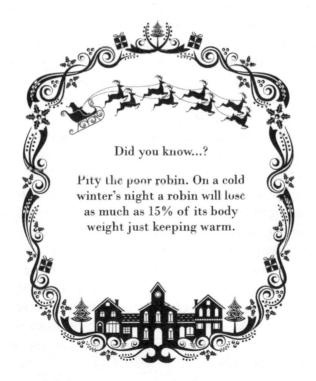

Did you know...?

Pity the poor robin. On a cold winter's night a robin will lose as much as 15% of its body weight just keeping warm.

is for Unprepared

Not matter how hard you try to be prepared, more often than not you'll find yourself braving the chaos of the Christmas Eve last minute shopping spree, either in order to pick up that essential festive gift for the dog or another jar of gravy powder.

But before you dash off to the local garage to buy that special someone another chocolate orange, bear in mind that if you've already left your Christmas shopping a little late, you risk paying up to 50% more than those people who are – how shall we put it? – a little better organised.

A survey of Christmas shoppers conducted in 2013 revealed that 16-24 year-olds are actually the most organised when it comes to getting the Christmas shopping done, with nearly 44% of them buying their festive gifts in, or even *before*, November! Those aged 45 or older are the ones who are more likely to leave it to the last minute with almost a third not even starting on the seasonal shop until the week before Christmas.

When you look at the gender of last minute shoppers, rather than their age, one quarter of men do most of their Christmas shopping at the last possible moment, while half of all women have it done before the first week of December.

15% of shoppers cashed in their store loyalty coupons and vouchers to cover the cost of their purchases, while one in ten of those surveyed planned so far ahead that they actually bought their first Christmas present for December 2013 in the January sales! The people surveyed made an average five trips to the shops to get their Christmas shopping done, while one in ten didn't shop in-store over the Christmas period at all, preferring to do so from the comfort of their laptop, tablet or smartphone!

Why do people kiss under the mistletoe?

Like so many others, stealing a kiss under the mistletoe is one of those traditions that are a hangover of our pre-Christian past. Both the Ancient Greeks and the druidic priests of the Celtic peoples revered the mistletoe, believing it to have supernatural healing properties. To the Romans the mistletoe was a symbol of peace and used as part of the Saturnalia celebrations.

Like other plants that remained green all year long, is was taken as a symbol of prosperity and fruitfulness. Thoughts of fertility returning to the land were foremost in the minds of the early peoples who relied on the bounteous gifts of the earth for their immediate survival, during the seemingly lifeless days of midwinter.

In Norse mythology, the plant was sacred to Frigga

(also known as Freya) who was the goddess of love. It was an arrow crafted from mistletoe wood that shot and killed Frigga's beloved son, Balder, the god of light, and this legend is just one possible source of the practice of kissing under the mistletoe. Following Balder's death, Frigga mourned his passing by sobbing her heart out. The tears that fell from her eyes transformed into the pearly white berries of the mistletoe. She then proceeded to kiss everyone who passed under the oak tree where the plant grew, instructing them that whenever they met beneath the mistletoe they should kiss one another in peace, rather than do each other harm.

As far as the Celtic druids were concerned, mistletoe only retained its magical properties if it was cut from a sacred oak where it grew using a golden sickle. It was then allowed to fall from the tree but was caught in a white cloth before it touched the ground. The fact that the plant grew completely off the ground was the reason for the druids' great respect for it. They imagined that because it apparently grew out of nothing it must have magical properties.

The name we know it by comes from two Anglo-Saxon words and reveals precisely how the mistletoe can grow where it does. *Mistel* is the Anglo-Saxon for 'dung' and *tan* means 'a small branch'. Birds (usually the mistle thrush) feast on the mistletoe's berries, then, having had their fill, they do what everyone does after a big meal – they void their bowels. The seeds excreted in this way germinate in the bark of the tree and a new mistletoe plant grows.

To complete the druids' ritual, two white bulls were sacrificed as a prayer was said. Quite a performance, but as far as the druids were concerned it was worth it. The mistletoe was called the 'all-healer'. Among its supposed powers were beliefs that it was a remedy against poison and that it made barren animals fertile again.

These beliefs persisted into Medieval times when it was fed to cattle to make sure they calved in the spring, and any woman hoping to fall pregnant would carry a sprig of it about her person. It was also considered an effective treatment for toothache, nervous disorders, epilepsy, heart disease and snakebites. It was somehow supposed to bring quarrels to an end, and was a sure means of protection against witches and lightning strikes! (One strongly-held belief had it that mistletoe was formed when lightning struck a tree.)

Today, mistletoe is becoming rarer in this country for, as well as oak, it particularly likes to grow on apple trees, and apple orchards have been shrinking in size and number throughout Britain over the last half century at an alarming rate. Much of the mistletoe you will see on sale at Christmas will have been imported from Normandy.

The more modern practice of kissing under the mistletoe can be traced back to eighteenth century England. Young women who stood underneath the mistletoe could not refuse a kiss, and if any unfortunate girl remained unkissed under the berries it was said that she would not marry during the coming year.

In one version of the custom, every time a young

man stole a kiss from a girl he plucked a berry from the mistletoe bough. When all the berries had been plucked, the privilege ceased, as is recalled by this ditty:

Pick a berry off the mistletoe

For ev'ry kiss that's given.

When the berries have all gone,

There's an end to the kissing.

At one stage, during the Medieval period, a new legend sprang up briefly that the cross on which Christ had been crucified was made from mistletoe – rather than holly, as a previous legend had stated – because at that time people believed the mistletoe had once been a tree itself. The story went that the mistletoe was so ashamed of the use to which it had been put that it shrank to become the parasitic plant we know today and, at the same time, was denied any contact with the ground. In Brittany, France, the plant is still known as *Herbe de la Croix* ('herb of the cross') because of this association.

It is likely that this legend drew from the Norse myth of the death of Balder, in which the mistletoe had then also been the innocent means of the Norse god's death. This attempt to Christianise the pagan mistletoe, however, was not successful and the plant was forbidden to be brought into any church building. The exception to this rule was York Minster, where a large bunch of mistletoe was laid on the altar every Christmas.

It was once the case that Christmas decorations,

including boughs of mistletoe, were treated with great respect. In Shropshire in particular it was considered extreme bad luck to throw them away – you didn't even dare let any piece fall onto the floor – and instead they were burnt or fed to cows. However, the mistletoe bough was carefully put away until it was time for a new one to replace it in twelve months' time. In this part of the country mistletoe was once associated with New Year rather than Christmas and was not put up until New Year's Eve.

> *Forth to the wood did merry-men go,*
>
> *To gather in the mistletoe.*
>
> (From 'Old Christmas' by Walter Scott)

The A to Z of Christmas

is for Vienna

Starting at the end of November and lasting until Christmas Day you will find a *Christkindlmärkte* on nearly every street corner in the Austrian city of Vienna. At these festive markets, small huts provide you with all manner of Christmas gifts, food and – most importantly – *Glühwein*, heated sweetened wine.

The *Christkindlmarkt* on the square in front of the City Hall, otherwise known as the *Rathausplatz*, is Vienna's quintessential classic Christmas Market. Strolling among the elaborately decorated trees in the park – including the '*Kasperl* tree' (or 'tree with seals'), and the '*Herzerlbaum*' ('Hearts tree'), as well as the so-called 'Post office in the clouds' – the Viennese and visitors from all over the world can enjoy the wonderful Christmas atmosphere.

The festively illuminated Schönbrunn Palace, the former summer residence of the Austrian Emperors, provides a spectacular backdrop for an idyllic Christmas village filled with the scent of mulled wine and gingerbread. And almost every day, festive concerts help to spread feelings of Christmas cheer.

In the Spittelberg historical quarter of the city, both traditional and original handicrafts are sold on the narrow paved alleyways, niches and courtyards, making it the most authentic of all Vienna's Christmas markets.

When did war stop for Christmas?

To be honest, war has stopped for Christmas on many occasions, but when people consider this question nowadays, the incident they usually call to mind is the Christmas truce of 1914.

During the Medieval period – the age of mass pitched battles and long, drawn-out sieges – the 'campaign season', as it was called, corresponded to the seasons of the year when there would be plentiful food on the ground, as well as relatively good weather; in other words, from spring through to autumn. As a result, it was very unlikely that you would be engaged in war with your enemies at the time of the winter feast.

By the nineteenth century, however, things had changed, and British soldiers found themselves far from hearth and home at Christmas during the Crimean War (1853-6), as well as both the First Anglo-Afghan War (1839-42) and the Second Afghan Campaign (1878-80). The Siege of the Sherpur Cantonment, a battle fought in December 1879, came to an end when troops stormed the military quarters in Kabul on 23 December, the day before Christmas Eve.

The First World War is notorious for many reasons, one of which being that when Britain first declared war on Germany in 1914 is was commonly believed that the fighting would be over by Christmas. Instead, this war of attrition would last for over four years and see more than nine million combatants killed.

The Christmas Truce is a term used to refer to a series of unofficial cessations of hostilities that occurred right along the Western Front during Christmas 1914. Soldiers had dug trenches and erected barbed wire to hold their positions from Lorraine in the south, as far as the English Channel in the north. In places the trenches were just yards apart, allowing the soldiers on one side to shout out to their enemies on the other; after a particularly heavy barrage, the soldiers even held up signs painted on wooden boards that said things like "Missed" or "Left a bit". This war-born black humour was the bizarre commencement of a conversation between the troops on both sides that would help bring the Christmas Truce about.

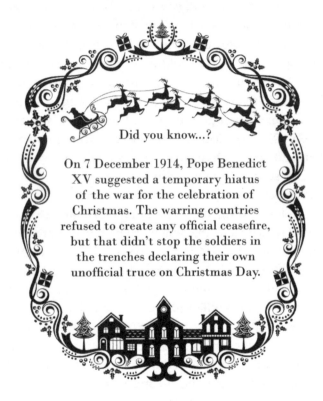

Did you know...?

On 7 December 1914, Pope Benedict XV suggested a temporary hiatus of the war for the celebration of Christmas. The warring countries refused to create any official ceasefire, but that didn't stop the soldiers in the trenches declaring their own unofficial truce on Christmas Day.

For most of the month of December 1914, the weather had been wet. But on Christmas Eve, a sharp drop in temperature resulted in the sort of white Christmas that usually only appears on Christmas cards. Germans celebrate Christmas on Christmas Eve, more than they do on 25 December, so on the Western Front on 24 December 1914, the German troops, hunkered down in their trenches, began to sing carols, and even went so far as to place Christmas trees lit with lanterns above the trenches. The following appeared in numerous UK newspapers after the event:

> Their trenches were a blaze of Christmas trees, and our sentries were regaled for hours with the traditional Christmas songs of the Fatherland. Their officers even expressed annoyance the next day that some of these trees had been fired on, insisting that they were part almost of the sacred rite.

What was to follow was so remarkable that hundreds of soldiers felt compelled to write home about that particular Christmas in the trenches after the event. The following is from a letter written by one Private H. Scrutton of the Essex Regiment, and published in the *Norfolk Chronicle* on 1 January 1915:

> As I told you before, our trenches are only 30 or 40 yards away from the Germans. This led to an exciting incident the other day. Our fellows have been in the habit of shouting across to the enemy and we used to get answers from them. We were told to get into conversation with them and this is what happened:
>
> From our trenches: "Good morning, Fritz." (No answer).
> "Good morning, Fritz." (Still no answer).
> "GOOD MORNING FRITZ!"
> From German trenches: "Good morning."
> From our trench: "How are you?"

"All right."

"Come over here, Fritz."

"No. If I come I get shot."

"No you won't. Come on."

"No fear."

"Come and get some fags, Fritz."

"No. You come half way and I meet you."

"All right."

One of our fellows thereupon stuffed his pocket with fags and got over the trench. The German got over his trench, and right enough they met half way and shook hands, Fitz taking the fags and giving cheese in exchange.

Rifleman C H Brazier, of Queen's Westminsters, of Bishop's Stortford, wrote this in a letter home, the extract later appearing in *The Hertfordshire Mercury*, on Saturday 9 January 1915:

You will no doubt be surprised to hear that we spent our Christmas in the trenches after all and that Christmas Day was a very happy one. On Christmas Eve the Germans entrenched opposite us began calling out to us 'Cigarettes', 'Pudding', 'A Happy Christmas' and 'English – means good', so two of our fellows climbed over the parapet of the trench and went towards the German trenches. Half-way they were met by four Germans, who said they would not shoot on Christmas Day if we did not. They gave our fellows cigars and a bottle of wine and were given a cake and cigarettes. When they came back I went out with some more of our fellows and we were met by about 30 Germans, who seemed to be very nice fellows. I got one of them to write his name and address on a postcard as a souvenir. All through the night we sang carols to them and they sang to us and one played 'God Save the King' on a mouth organ.

The famous truce did not happen everywhere. Some parts of the Western Front still experienced heavy shelling and firing on Christmas Day, and there were further fatalities. In January 1915, the *Hampshire Chronicle* published this, written by Pat Collard to his parents at The Chestnut Horse pub at Easton near Winchester:

Perhaps you read of the conversation on Christmas Day between us and the Germans. It's all lies. The sniping went on just the same; in fact, our captain was wounded, so don't believe what you see in the papers.

But in many places on and around Christmas Day 1914, the sounds of rifles firing and shells exploding faded, to be replaced by sounds of seasonal celebrations and gestures of goodwill between men whom the actions of foolish old men thousands of miles away had made enemies.

German and British troops sang Christmas carols to each other across No Man's Land, and Allied soldiers even reported hearing brass bands joining the Germans in their singing. And then, at first light on Christmas Day, some soldiers left the protection of the trenches to wish their fellow man Merry Christmas – the Germans doing so in English, the native tongue of their sworn enemies – to exchange presents of cigarettes and plum puddings, while others made the most of the unexpected ceasefire to recover the bodies of their comrades who had fallen, during earlier raids, in No Man's Land.

But the most famous incident of the unofficial truce has to be the football match that took place between the German and British forces on Christmas Day, on the front line between Frelinghien and Houplines. Using caps for goalposts (rather than jumpers) German soldiers of the 133rd Royal Saxon Regiment took on a team from the Scottish Seaforth Highlanders. The game lasted for an hour, until the German Commanding Officer heard about it and ordered that it should cease. While some say that no one kept score, others later reported that the score was 3-2… to Germany.

Unfortunately the truce could not last and would never be repeated, with future attempts at holiday ceasefires being quashed by officers' threats of disciplinary action. As Lance-Corporal Henderson of the Royal Engineers was reported as saying of the day after that memorable and moving Christmas (in *The Hampshire Chronicle* on 30 January 1915):

> The alarm went about midnight, and we
> stood up till daybreak, when we found that

our pals of the previous two days had tried to rush our position, but they got cut up as usual, and I believe the next morning the ground where we had been so chummy, and where Germans had wished us a merry Christmas, was now covered with their dead.

Did you know...?

'Pipes of Peace' is a song written by former Beatle Sir Paul McCartney, released on 5 December 1983, which went on to become number one in not just the UK but also many other countries around the world. The video to accompany the single was shot at Chobham Common, in Surrey. It recreated the famous 1914 football match and featured over 100 extras. McCartney played the parts of both a British and a German soldier – who meet in No Man's Land, exchanging photos of their loved ones while their fellow men socialise over a kickabout – even going so far as to have his famously flowing locks cut short for added realism.

The public reaction to news of the Christmas Truce was one of excitement and wonderment. However, an anonymous letter published in *The Aberdeen Daily Journal*, on 9 January 1915, criticised the ceasefire:

> Fie on ye, Scotsmen! There is not much of
> the boasted Highland Pride left in you when
> you would sell it for a German souvenir.

Although it was widely understood that the truce was an aberration, and despite its detractors, the enduring legacy of the truce has been a positive one, and it is seen today as a fine example of humanity prevailing during one of the darkest hours in its long history. It has gone on to inspire songs, literature, films and works of art, but surely its greatest gift has been the message of hope, given to all mankind at Christmas time.

──────── **The A to Z of Christmas** ────────

is for Winter Solstice

21 December is traditionally the date of the Winter Solstice, the year's longest night and shortest day, and sometimes referred to as Yule. (The word 'solstice' derives from Latin *sol*, meaning 'sun', and *sistere*, 'to stand still'.) The winter solstice occurs at the instant when the Sun's position in the sky is at its greatest angular distance on the other side of the equatorial plane from the observer's hemisphere. Depending on the shift of the calendar, the event of the winter solstice occurs some time between 20 December and 23 December each year in the northern hemisphere.

The seasonal significance of the winter solstice is in the reversal of the gradually lengthening nights and shortening days. How cultures interpret this is varied, since it is sometimes said to astronomically mark either the beginning or middle of a hemisphere's winter. Though the winter solstice lasts an instant, the term is also colloquially used to refer to the full twenty-four hour period of the day on which it occurs. Worldwide, interpretation of the event has varied from culture to culture, but most have held a recognition of rebirth, involving holidays, festivals, gatherings and other ritual celebrations around that time.

Saint Thomas' Day is also celebrated on 21 December. Saint Thomas is commemorated on this day because he was the last one of the apostles to become convinced of Jesus' resurrection – in other words, he was the one who for the longest time remained in the 'night of unbelief and doubt.' He is also supposedly to have died on this day circa AD 72, near Chennai in India.

There are various traditions practised on this day, particularly in Germany, including the *Thomasfaulpelz* or *Domesel*, and the Rittberg wedding. *Thomasfaulpelz* or *Domesel* (the 'lazybone' or 'donkey' of Saint Thomas Day) were names given to the last person to get out of bed and for the last student to appear in class on that particular morning in Westphalia (roughly the region between the Rivers Rhine and Weser, located north of the Ruhr River). The *Rittburgische Hochzeit* (Rittberg wedding), also in Westphalia, was an opulent meal served in the belief that if you ate well on Saint Thomas Day, you could expect to do so all of the next year.

Why do people build snowmen at Christmas time?

The creation of anthropomorphic sculptures formed from atmospheric water vapour frozen into ice crystals – more commonly known as a snowmen – is a popular pastime during the winter months when (or even if) it snows. Your typical snowman is made from two or three large snowballs, with sticks, pieces of coal, vegetables, and items of clothing being added to help create the illusion that they are in fact people.

There are documented records of snowmen being built since Medieval times – the earliest being an illustration in the margin of one of the pages of the 1380 *Book of Hours*, that resides in Koninklijke Bibliotheek, in The Hague – but it is likely that the practice dates back to the Neolithic period. After all, the representation of the human form, in no matter what medium, is as old as human beings themselves. Since Neolithic peoples painted the inside of caves with scenes of hunts, as well as those of everyday life, and stone age artists carved sculptures of the Earth Goddesses from the material that gave them their name, why wouldn't they also have used snow to create effigies of the human form (when the weather conditions permitted)?

As snow can be sculpted without the need for tools, it would have been a very appealing material to work in. Ice-age man sought to create images of the idealised human form, which for him meant the maternal, female form – the voluptuous, well-endowed shape of Mother Earth herself. So it is highly likely that the snow sculptures we describe as snowmen actually started out as snowwomen. (It's uncertain when snowballs were introduced.)

25,000 years later, and we're still building human figures out of snow, but only if the snow is of the right consistency. As it approaches its melting point snow becomes moist and is more easily compacted, allowing for the construction of large snowballs simply by rolling. Powdered snow will not stick to itself and so is not an ideal building material for snowmen. The best time to build a snowman is the next warm afternoon following a heavy snowfall.

The snowman doubtless became a part of the Christmas festivities, not just because of the wintery time of year at which those celebrations took place, but as part of Christianity's mass assimilation of seasonal pagan practices, such as the Christmas tree and Father Christmas.

Did you know...?

The tallest snowman ever created was built in the US town of Bethel, in Maine, in 1999. Called Angus, King of the Mountain, the effigy stood almost 35 metres tall (at 113 feet, 7 inches), weighed over 4,082,331 kg (9,000,000 lbs) and was made up of 5,663 cubic metres (or 200,000 cubic feet) of snow. Angus had huge Christmas wreathes for eyes, his carrot nose was a construction of chicken wire and muslin 2 m (6 ft) in length, and six car tyres were used to create his mouth. He even had a fleece hat, a fleece scarf 36.5 m (120 ft) long, and two 3 m (10 ft) tall Christmas trees for arms. Construction was completed in February 1999, and Angus didn't melt until four months later, on 10 June.

Some scholars have linked the creation of snow effigies to the worship of Jack Frost, or at least the nature spirits from which he is descended. A variant form of Old Man Winter, Jack Frost is the personification of frost, ice, snow, sleet, and freezing cold weather. (In Russia he is the rather more severe Grandfather Frost.) He is the one supposedly responsible for changing the colour of autumn foliage, and for painting the fern-like patterns of ice seen on cold window panes in the depths of winter. Although originally a sinister mischief maker, in recent years he has been transformed into a kindly, child-like sprite who simply wishes to enjoy himself and bring happiness to others, as in the 2012 Christmas movie *Rise of the Guardians*.

Of course the name 'Frosty' has also long been associated with snowmen, or at least one snowman in particular. The popular song 'Frosty the Snowman' was written by Walter 'Jack' Rollins and Steve Nelson, and was first recorded by 'the singing cowboy' Gene Autry, and his backing band the Cass County Boys, in 1950. It tells the story of a snowman that is brought to life by means of a magical top hat, which a group of children place on his head. The song ends with Frosty being forced to leave town as the warm glare of the sun becomes too much for him, but promising that he will be back again, someday. The song was set in Armonk, New York, and every year Armonk has a parade dedicated to Frosty.

The recording of 'Frosty the Snowman' was a calculated move to follow up the success of Autry's recording of 'Rudolph the Red-Nosed Reindeer' the previous year. 'Frosty' has since been subject to various adaptations into other media, including the 1950 children's book *Frosty the Snow Man*, and a popular television special made in 1969.

The UK has its own snowman story that appears in the television schedules every Christmas. Called simply *The Snowman*, it is an adaptation of the wordless picture book of the same name, written and drawn by English author Raymond Briggs in 1978. In 1982, the book was turned into a 26-minute animated film, which debuted on British television on Boxing Day that year. The film featured the song 'Walking in the Air' which was made famous by Aled Jones, then a choirboy, who had a number 5 hit with it in the UK charts in 1985. (The song is also ranked as thirtieth on the list of All-Time Biggest Hits About Christmas and The Festive Season.) However, the version of the song used on the film soundtrack was not sung by Aled Jones at all, but by another chorister, Peter Auty. Auty was not credited in the original version of *The Snowman*, a severe oversight that was not put right until the 20th anniversary version was released in 2002.

In 2012 *The Snowman* received a sequel. Called *The Snowman and the Snowdog*, the 23-minute animated film first aired on Channel 4, on Christmas Eve, to celebrate the thirtieth anniversary of the original short and of the television station itself. Many of the original team returned to work on the sequel which was made using the same traditional techniques as the original. These consisted of drawing onto pieces of celluloid with pastels, crayons and other colouring tools.

Disney's 2013 holiday movie *Frozen*, based loosely on Hans Christian Andersen's *The Snow Queen*, featured an animated snowman (in every sense of the word) called Olaf. The 3D computer-animated musical fantasy comedy-drama used snowflake generating software to produce a total of 2,000 different snowflakes, which are seen throughout the course of the entire film, and depending on the shot in question, it could take up to 4,000 computers thirty hours just to complete one frame.

The character of Olaf (whose name is Nordic for 'treasure' and pronounced 'oh, laugh') was given a childlike innocence, whilst also clearly being the comedic relief in the movie. He was voiced by Josh Gad, an American actor who won the Annie Award for 'Outstanding Achievement in Voice Acting in an Animated Feature Production' at the forty-first Annie Awards in 2014.

It is likely that Olaf was inspired by another Hans Christian Andersen fairy tale, called *The Snowman*, in which the eponymous snowman falls in love with a warm stove but cannot be with it because it would cause him to melt.

Did you know...?

When your granny used to say, "Ooh, it's too cold for snow!" she wasn't just passing on some old wives' tale – she was actually telling the truth. Since snow is frozen water, if there are not enough water droplets in the air it cannot snow; simple as that. As a result, the driest place on Earth isn't in the Sahara Desert, or Death Valley in California. It's actually a place known as the Dry Valleys and it is in Antarctica. The area is completely free of ice and snow, and it never rains there at all! In fact, parts of the Antarctic continent haven't seen any rain for around 2 million years! But Antarctica is also the wettest place in world, due to the fact that 70% of the Earth's fresh water is found there in the form of ice.

10 things you probably didn't know about snow

1. The average snowflake has a top speed of 1.7 m (5.5 ft) per second.

2. For it to snow, the tops of the clouds must be below zero degrees Celsius (or 32 degrees Fahrenheit).

3. The largest snowflake ever observed supposedly appeared on 28 January 1887, in Fort Keogh, Montana (USA). It was reportedly, "15 inches wide and 8 inches thick". However, this record seems to be based on the word of a ranch owner named Matt Coleman, who described the snowflake as "larger than milk pans" to the Monthly Weather Review journal at the time.

4. Permanent snow and ice cover about 12% of the Earth's land surface, while Mt Kilimanjaro in Tanzania is the only permanent snowcap within sight of the equator.

5. Photokeratitis (more commonly known as snow blindness) is caused because snow reflects a high level of ultraviolet radiation that can be hazardous to human eyes. Sunglasses, goggles and other eye protection help absorb the harmful UV rays.

6. 80% of the world's fresh water is locked up as ice or snow.

7. A single snowstorm can drop 40 million tons of snow, carrying the energy equivalent to 120 atom bombs.

8. There is not a law of nature that prohibits two snowflakes from being identical.

9. In Australia, snowfalls are common above 1,500 m (4,921 ft) in the Alps (part of the Great Dividing Range) during the winter, but there are no permanent snowfields anywhere on the continent.

10. The most snow produced in a single snowstorm is 4.8 m (15.75 ft) at Mt Shasta Ski Bowl, California (USA) between 13 and 19 February 1959. However, the highest snowfall ever recorded in a one year period was 31.1 m (102 ft) in Mount Rainier, Washington State (also in the USA), between 19 February 1971 and 18 February 1972.

If you're feeling a little on the chilly side after reading all those snowy facts, why not sit down in front of a crackling fire and enjoy a Snowball? Of the alcoholic variety...

Snowball Cocktail

2 oz Advocaat
Top up lemonade

1/2 oz fresh lime juice

Mix all the ingredients in a cocktail shaker and pour into an unusually shaped glass. Add crushed ice and decorations for a little extra festive sparkle.

The A to Z of Christmas

is for Xmas

Xmas (sometimes 'X-mas') is a common abbreviated form of Christmas, usually pronounced 'eks-mas'. Because it removes the word Christ from Christmas, some people believe it to be irreverent, but how did such a practice come about?

In fact, it dates back further than you might suspect, and has nothing to do with devaluing the Christian festival at all. In reality, both Christ and Christmas have been abbreviated for at least 1,000 years. The word Christ appears in Medieval documents as both 'XP' and 'Xt' and can even be found in this form in the Anglo-Saxon Chronicle from 1021. But why were those particular letters used?

Some believe the 'X' is used as a symbol of the cross on which Christ died, but it is not the case. For early Christians, simply *being* a Christian was a dangerous business. The persecution of those who professed to the worship of Christ by the Romans was at its height, and the stories of Christians being thrown to the lions in Rome's Coliseum have become the stuff of notorious legend.

To live and worship in such times required no small amount of subterfuge on the part of early Christians. To communicate with other like-minded individuals they employed all sorts of signs and symbols which, to the uninitiated, would have meant nothing. These signs and symbols included the fish (employed because the letters of the Greek word for fish *ichthys* taken in order were the initial letters of the acronym Ἰησοῦς Χριστός, Θεοῦ Υἱός, Σωτήρ meaning 'Jesus Christ, God's Son, Saviour') and the *labrum*, made up of the letters 'X' and 'P'.

'X' and 'P' are the capital forms of the first two letters of the Greek spelling of Christ (or Χριστός) and, as a result, should be pronounced 'chi' and 'rho'. These two letters are often seen merged together, with one letter over the top of the other, in the form of the *labrum*, in churches around the world, particularly those of the Catholic, Protestant and Orthodox denominations.

By the fifteenth century, 'Xmas' was widely used as an abbreviation of 'Christmas', in part due to the invention of the printing press by Johannes Gutenberg, in around 1436. This new-fangled machine used moveable type, giving the printer much greater flexibility and a quicker work rate. That said, to set the type was still a tedious, time-consuming and expensive job as it was completed by hand. As a result abbreviations were common in all manner of publications, including religious ones.

In fact, the Church itself used the capital letter 'X' in place of the word Christ, to cut the printing costs of books and pamphlets. Newspapers and other publications followed suit, substituting not only 'X' for 'Christ' and 'Xmas' for 'Christmas', but also 'Xian' for 'Christian' and 'Xianity' for – you guessed it – 'Christianity'.

So you can see, the use of 'Xmas' in place of 'Christmas' is not solely a modern practice and it is certainly not part of a conspiracy to cross Christ out of the festive season, or for secular, commercially driven celebrations to usurp the Christian holiday. It is simply another of those ancient Christmas traditions that has been forgotten with the passage of time.

What are the Twelve Days of Christmas?

It is one of the most popular Christmas carols, telling of a zealous suitor's extravagant Christmas gifts to his sweetheart. But when do the actual twelve days of Christmas fall, and what is the true meaning of the carol's bizarre shopping list?

Let's start with the twelve days of Christmas themselves. Many people have come to believe that the twelve days of Christmas are those leading up to the main event on 25 December. However, they are actually the days that come after it, with the last day being Epiphany (the date on which the Christian Church celebrates the visit of the Magi to the Christ child), which falls on 6 January, and is why that date is also known as Twelfth Night.

This period of time has come to be known as both Twelve-tide and Christmastide. In Medieval England, it was a time of continuous feasting and merrymaking. There was always plenty of food to go round; at least there was plenty of meat to go round, as most animals were slaughtered come the winter to save the farmers the cost of having to feed them during the long winter months.

But what of the carol? There is a widely perpetuated myth that 'The Twelve Days of Christmas' was one of the so-called catechism songs. The theory goes that during the period 1558–1829 – when it was illegal to worship as a Catholic, with laws in place preventing people from either publically or privately practising the faith of the Roman Church – certain songs were written with the express intention of teaching young Catholics the basic tenets of their faith, and some people believe that 'The Twelve Days of Christmas' is one of these.

These believers insist that each of the otherwise frankly ludicrous gifts is a coded message representing a significant element of the Catholic catechism. In this case, the partridge in the pear tree is Jesus on the cross, the two turtle doves are the Old and New Testaments, while the three French hens represent the gifts of the Spirit mentioned in the first book of Corinthians – faith, hope and love. The four calling birds are in fact the evangelists – Matthew, Mark, Luke and John – the writers of the Gospels, and the five gold rings become the Jewish Torah, the first five books of the Bible which contained the laws that Jewish people should live by.

It goes on; the six geese a-laying are the six days of creation while the seven swans a-swimming are the seven gifts of the Holy Spirit – wisdom, understanding, counsel, fortitude, knowledge, piety and fear of the Lord God. The eight maids-a-milking stand in for the eight beatitudes mentioned by Jesus in the Sermon on the Mount. The nine ladies dancing are the nine fruits of the Spirit listed in the Book of Galatians – love, joy, peace, patience, kindness, goodness, faithfulness, gentleness and self-control – and the ten lords-a-leaping are in fact the Ten Commandments. The eleven pipers piping are the eleven faithful apostles (so don't include the traitorous Judas), and the twelve drummers drumming are the twelve points of belief expressed in the Apostles' Creed.

Only they don't mean that, not any of them, at least according to others. The truth is that there isn't any substantive evidence to either support the Catholic-teaching claim or to disprove it. What we do know is that the carol was a part of Christmas traditions in Europe and Scandinavia from as early as the sixteenth century.

The familiar words of 'The Twelve Days of Christmas' were also published in London, around the year 1780, in a collection of children's rhymes called *Mirth without Mischief*. It was included in this context as a memory game with accompanying forfeits for the forgetful.

It's not just the origin and purpose of the carol that are a cause of confusion; the words themselves are even up for debate. In certain versions of the carol, the gifts of the last four days appear in a different order. Instead of nine ladies dancing, ten lords a-leaping, eleven pipers piping and twelve drummers drumming you could have nine drummers drumming, ten pipers piping, eleven ladies, or even dames, a-dancing, and the twelve lords a-leaping. There is even one variation in which ten fiddlers fiddle, so doing the pipers out of a job.

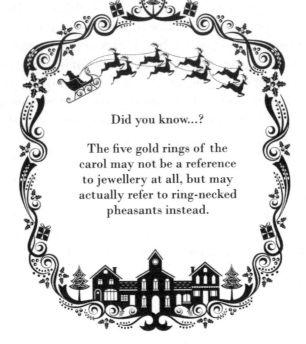

Did you know...?

The five gold rings of the carol may not be a reference to jewellery at all, but may actually refer to ring-necked pheasants instead.

The four calling birds can also be a problem. In some versions they are mockingbirds while in others they are colly birds, an Old English name for blackbirds. There is even some debate over the stalwart partridge, or at least its pear tree. The French for partridge is *perdrix* (pronounced *per-dree*) which could actually have made the original opening line, 'A partridge, *une perdrix*.'

Whatever the origins of the carol, 'The Twelve Days of Christmas' is the source of much amusement in that it provides the basis for a suitably festive mathematical

Did you know...?

There is a mathematical formula you can use to work out the total number of gifts given by the extravagant 'my true love' celebrated in 'The Twelve Days of Christmas' on any one day of the twelve days. Where N is a particular day out of the twelve, the total number of gifts given on that day = $N(N+1)(N+2)/6$.

brainteaser, that of 'How many gifts does the young lady, who narrates the carol, receive?' The gifts sent by the eager suitor referred to as 'my true love' are cumulative. The lucky lady receiving them doesn't just receive a partridge in a pear tree on day one and then two turtle doves the next. Looking at the lyrics closely it soon becomes apparent that on day two his sweetheart receives two turtle doves and *another* partridge. On the third day of Christmas she gets the French hens, another pair of turtle doves and yet another partridge, pear tree, the works. And so it goes on...

Rather than receiving a total of 78 gifts over the twelve days, the narrator of the carol actually receives 364 individual items, one for each day of a traditional year, minus Christmas Day.

People have had some fun with this over the years. Since 1984, PNC Wealth Management based in the US has maintained the Christmas Price Index. This is a pricing chart that plots the current cost of one set of each of the gifts given by the True Love of the carol. This has even been used as a more general economic indicator. However, it is also used to calculate the True Cost of Christmas, in other words the total cumulative cost of all the gifts listed, including repetitions. (The people mentioned in the song are hired, not purchased.)

According to PNC, in 1984 the True Cost of Christmas for the romantically inclined was $61,318.94. However by 2007 it had risen to $114,651.18, which is equivalent to roughly £67,093.87.

Did you know...?

The Mesopotamian holiday of Zagmuk lasted for twelve days and featured the symbolic sacrifice of the king (replaced by a convenient convict) which compensated for the sins of the people. Sound familiar?

The A to Z of Christmas

is for Yule

To our pagan ancestors living in the frozen north of Europe and Scandinavia, the dark days of winter were a frightening time. The darkness was the domain of demons and malicious spirits. On top of that, Odin, chief among the Norse gods, flew through the sky on his eight-legged horse Sleipnir, looking down at the world with his furious one-eyed gaze, deciding who should prosper and who should perish in the year ahead.

Yule was the name given to the Viking festive feast, a time when light and new birth were celebrated in the face of darkness and death as witnessed in the natural world. It was at this time that evergreens were brought into the house; a sign that life persisted, even during these darkest days of the year.

The English word Yule is a corruption of the Old Norse *Jōl*. However, *Jōl* itself may derive from *hjól*, meaning 'wheel'. In this sense, it refers to the moment when the wheel of the year is at its lowest point, in midwinter, ready to rise again in the spring.

What is a Yule log?

The Yule log, either in the form of a small wood and holly sprig centrepiece placed on the table during Christmas dinner, or in its guise as a chocolate dessert, is still a popular part of Christmas, particularly among those with a sweet tooth.

To those people living in the cold climes of northern Europe and Scandinavia in centuries past, winter was a dangerous time. The sensible choice was to stay inside at this time of year, safe from the myriad imagined horrors that lurked outside (and to avoid dying from exposure). To help keep the darkness at bay, on or around the 21 December, the time of the winter solstice, fathers and sons would go out into the forests and bring back the largest log they could find. This massive piece of timber was then put on the fire and left to burn for the entirety of the season of Yule – twelve days altogether.

However, despite the deeply felt need to keep unwanted spirits outside, in Scandinavia people also believed that the burning Yule log warmed the frozen shades of the family's dearly-departed, who returned to the ancestral home every Christmas Eve. Some families even went to the trouble of laying a place for them at the dinner table.

In England, the preferred wood for the Yule log was ash, while in Scotland birch was favoured. As well as keeping everyone warm and providing heat to cook by, the Yule log was also a symbol of prosperity to come; every spark that fell from it was supposed to represent a pig or calf to be born in the spring.

In Germany, the Yule log miraculously had the power to protect a home from lightning, and whenever a storm threatened, the stump of the *Christbrand* (as it was called in Germany after the country's conversion to Christianity) was re-kindled.

As long as the Yule log burned, feasting and revelry were in order. But should the log go out, then bad fortune would fall upon the household, for it was then that Old Night and its minions would sneak inside to do their mischief.

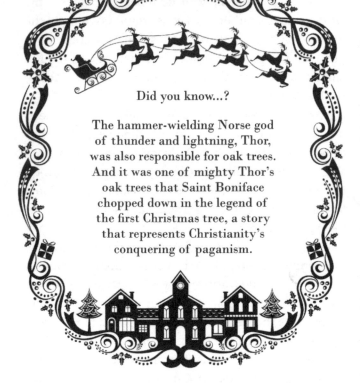

Did you know...?

The hammer-wielding Norse god of thunder and lightning, Thor, was also responsible for oak trees. And it was one of mighty Thor's oak trees that Saint Boniface chopped down in the legend of the first Christmas tree, a story that represents Christianity's conquering of paganism.

Despite the Christianising of the winter solstice, the Yule log remained an important feature of the festive season. The old gods might have gone, replaced by Christianity, but the ancient superstitious fears surrounding the dark had not!

To the Celtic mind, when the days were at their shortest, at the end of December, the sun itself stood still and it was only by keeping the Yule log burning for those twelve days that the sun would deem to return and the days grow longer once more. So it was that by the Middle Ages the log would be hauled into the house on Christmas Eve, with great pomp and ceremony, and lit using a piece of the previous year's log, saved for just this purpose.

By the nineteenth century in England the custom changed, as so many did under the influence of the more practically-minded Victorians. Now, rather than burning for twelve days, the Yule log only had to last twelve hours, and in some homes the log was replaced by a candle (candles having their own symbolic connections with the Star of Bethlehem).

Of course, in our day and age, the Yule log has become the edible Christmas log. For any chocolate lover it has to be one of the highlights of the festive fare that gets wheeled out – better even than Christmas cake! And if you're one such admirer of the cocoa bean, then you should try this recipe yourself.

Chocolate Christmas Log

175 g/6 oz butter
175 g/6 oz plain chocolate
140 ml/¼ pint of double cream
100 g/3½ oz caster sugar
75 g/3 oz plain flour
75 g/3 oz icing sugar

4 eggs
4 tbs rum
1 tbs cocoa powder
1 tbs vanilla essence

2 drops almond essence
Icing sugar

Start by greasing and lining a 33 x 22 cm (13 x 9 inch) Swiss roll tin and pre-heat the oven to 200°C. Cream the eggs and sugar together in a large bowl before folding in the sieved flour and cocoa powder. Transfer the whole lot to the tin and bake for 12–15 minutes, until the cake has risen and turned golden. Take it out and allow to cool, but only slightly.

Place a sheet of greaseproof paper on a dampened cloth and sprinkle caster sugar on it. Turn the cake out onto the sheet, trim the edges and roll it up. Allow the cake to cool further. Then, whisk together the double cream, rum and both the vanilla and almond essence until stiff. Gently unroll the cake again and spread it with the cream filling. Roll it up once more.

Cream together the butter, icing sugar and chocolate, then cover the cake with the mixture. Sprinkle your finished chocolate log with icing sugar and chill in the fridge for one hour before serving. Garnish with a sprig of holly.

What is Twelfth Night?

Apart from a comedy by England's greatest playwright, William Shakespeare, you mean?

Twelfth Night falls on 6 January at the end of the traditional Twelve Days of Christmas. And 6 January just happens to be the feast of the Epiphany. The Epiphany was the manifestation of the Christ to the three kings, in other words the occasion when the three wise men came before the infant Jesus and paid him homage, giving him their gifts of gold, frankincense and myrrh.

The feast of the Epiphany originated in the East during the third century, in honour of Christ's baptism, but by the fourth century it had become part of Western tradition and was associated with Christ's appearance to the non-Jewish community (or Gentiles) as represented by the Magi, who were visitors from foreign lands.

From the time of William the Conqueror up until the start of the seventeenth century, the feast of the Epiphany was celebrated much more lavishly than Christmas Day. This is because the feast day was associated with the idea of kingship and majesty. For many years it was the custom to exchange gifts on the Epiphany, rather than the celebration of the feast of the Nativity.

Today, this once favoured feast is barely celebrated at all, instead becoming a rather gloomy affair, an anti-climax of a day when the Christmas tree, cards and other decorations are taken down. However, there are some Twelfth Night traditions which have lasted the test of time and that are still practised today.

One of these is the service held at St James's Palace, London, attended by the Royal Family. At this service, members of the Royal Household present the Chapel Royal with the three gifts brought to the Christ child by the Magi. Another tradition, upheld by the cast of the play currently being performed at the Theatre Royal Drury Lane at that time, is the eating of the Baddeley Cake. This is as a result of a stipulation made in the last will and testament of one Robert Baddeley, an actor from the eighteenth century, after whom the cake is named. In the West of England, Twelfth Night is the time when wassailing ceremonies are carried out.

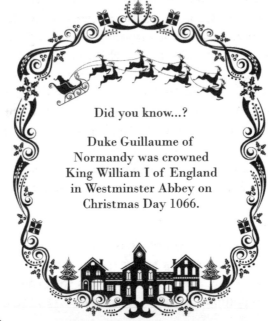

Did you know...?

Duke Guillaume of Normandy was crowned King William I of England in Westminster Abbey on Christmas Day 1066.

At one time in England, Twelfth Night was known as being a good occasion on which to carry out various good luck rituals, as well as for its religious processions which almost went hand-in-hand with the spirited, and good humoured, revels. Some of these rituals were linked to the countryside and farming, seeing as how, in England's past, people's lives were so strongly connected to the land and the ever-changing seasons. One of them had farmers lighting bonfires to drive evil spirits away from their farms and fields, the drunken agriculturalists cheering as they circled the fires to hasten the hobgoblins on their way.

Did you know...?

The title of William Shakespeare's *Twelfth Night, or What You Will*, makes reference to the Twelfth Night tradition of servants dressing up as their masters, men as women, and so forth. In it, the heroine Viola dresses up and masquerades as a man. Like many of Shakespeare's comedies, its humour centres on a case of mistaken identity.

There was also the time-honoured guessing game, whereby the (now probably inebriated) farmer had to guess what was being roasted in the kitchen before being permitted to re-enter his own home. This was not as easy as it might sound because his good wife might have something as ridiculously inedible as a shoe turning on the spit.

And then there were the Morris men dancing in the streets, as well as fools, hobby-horses and all. Practical jokes were the name of the game on Twelfth Night and the playing of games – particularly games of chance – with everyone determined to make the most of the last day of the holiday season.

Having taken down the Christmas cards and decorations for another year, Twelfth Night presented one last opportunity for a knees-up, the highlight being the cutting of the twelfth-cake. The renowned diarist Samuel Pepys wrote about the celebrations in his household. In an entry from 1668 he writes of offering his guests, 'an excellent cake which cost me near 20 shillings, of our Jane's making, which was cut into twenty pieces, there being by that time so many of our company'. Once everyone had enjoyed the cake made by Pepys' servant, they partied until 2 a.m., dancing and singing. The diarist also mentions that his neighbours joined them in this carousing, but then, from the sounds of it, they probably had little choice. It was either go round to the Pepyses' and join in the fun or spend a sleepless night in bed being kept awake by the party going on next door!

The traditional Twelfth Night cake was supposed to have a dried pea or bean hidden somewhere inside it. Whoever found the bean was proclaimed king or queen for the rest of the evening's fun and frivolity. It then became their responsibility to announce the toasts and lead everyone else in the drinking that ensued. However, some kings and queens also earned themselves the responsibility of covering the bill the next day. In time, the bean became a silver sixpence which was cooked inside the Christmas pudding rather than the cake.

Twelfth-Cake

175 g/6 oz flour

175 g/6 oz butter

175 g/6 oz sugar

3 eggs

3 tbs brandy

340 g/12 oz currants

40 g/1½ oz flaked almonds

25 g/1 oz orange and lemon peel, finely chopped

1 tbs honey

1 tsp of vinegar

Soften the butter and add to the sugar and cream in a mixing bowl. Cream the mixture until light and fluffy. Add the eggs, one at a time, beating well; also add a tablespoon of flour to stop them curdling. Pour in the brandy, followed by the flour and then the spices. Fold them all in, keeping the mixture light and airy. Lastly stir in the currants, almonds, peel and honey. The mixture needs to be poured into a prepared cake tin which is when you can also add a pea or bean, if you wish (but **do not** use a kidney bean as if it is undercooked it can prove toxic!). Bake for two hours until the cake has browned on top.

The baking of the twelfth-cake brought out the competitive natures of London shopkeepers during the nineteenth century, with rival firms trying to outdo each other in terms of quantity as much as quality. In 1811, one Adams of Cheapside made the bold claim that his cake, 'considerably surpasses in size any that has hitherto been made in London, or in fact the world'. He went on to say that the monster confection weighed close to half a ton and had been made using, 'two and a half hundredweight of currants and upwards of a thousand eggs'.

However, the twelfth-cake had had its day and the tradition was beginning to die out around the country. Instead it was replaced by the Christmas cake which actually made use of many of the same ingredients.

One of the last twelfth-cakes was made for Queen

Victoria by one Mr Mawditt, the First Yeoman of the
Confectionary in 1849. It was decorated with a scene
of an eighteenth century picnic. However, it was
Queen Victoria who helped set the trend for large,
rich fruitcakes. The firm of Gunter and Wand made
her such a cake for her wedding in February 1840, and
so it became popular to have rich fruitcakes made for
weddings in general. However, it is unlikely that those

that came after Victoria's were ten feet in diameter! Another hundred smaller cakes were also made for Victoria and Albert's wedding which were given to the royal couple's friends.

Mrs Beeton (1836-65) is arguably one of the most famous cookery writers in history and amongst the many recipes she has handed down to us, is one for that most seasonal of treats. So rather than using the handwritten recipe handed down from your grandmother this year, why not try Mrs Beeton's take on the cake for a change?

Mrs Beeton's Christmas Cake

5 cups of flour

1 cup of melted butter

1 cup of cream

1 cup of treacle

1 cup of moist sugar

2 eggs

15 g/½ oz of powdered ginger

225 g/½ lb of raisins

1 tsp of carbonate of soda

1 tsp of vinegar

Put the flour, sugar, ginger and raisins into
a basin and mix these dry ingredients together

thoroughly. Then stir in the melted butter, cream, treacle and well-whisked eggs. Beat the mixture for a few minutes. Dissolve the soda in the vinegar, add it to the dough, and mix the whole lot together well. Spoon the mixture into a well-greased cake tin and bake it in a moderate oven for 1¾–2¼ hours.

The A to Z of Christmas

is for Zoophagous

Christmas Day 1870 saw the city of Paris under siege by the Prussian army. However, the fact that the enemy had stopped any food getting into the city for 99 days (and counting), wasn't going to stop Café Voisin, 261 rue Saint-Honoré, from serving a fabulous, slap-up Christmas dinner. If you had been fortunate (or unfortunate) enough to be there yourself you would have enjoyed the following splendid repast:

Hors-d'oeuvres

Buttered Radishes, Stuffed Donkey's Head, Sardines

Soups

Purée of Red Beans with Croûtons

Elephant Consummé

Entrées

Fried Gudgeons, Roast Camel English Style

Jugged Kangaroo

Roast Bear Chops au Poivre

Roasts

Haunch of Wolf, Venison Sauce

Cat Flanked by Rats

Watercress Salad

Antelope Terrine with Truffles

Mushroom Bordelaise

Buttered Green Peas

Dessert

Rice Cake with Jam

Gruyère Cheese

Wines

First service

Latour Blanche 1861

Château Palmer 1864

Second service

Mouton Rothschild 1846

Romanee Conti 1858

Grand Porto 1827

And where did they get all the fresh meat from? Let's just say that a trip to the zoo on Boxing Day would have been a bit of a let-down.

Our revels now are ended

So we keep the olden greeting
With its meaning deep and true,
And wish a merrie Christmas
And a happy New Year to you.

(Old English saying)